Tar Heels in Gray

Tar Heels in Gray

*Life in the 30th North Carolina
Infantry in the Civil War*

JOHN B. CAMERON

McFarland & Company, Inc., Publishers
Jefferson, North Carolina

This book has undergone peer review.

LIBRARY OF CONGRESS CATALOGUING-IN-PUBLICATION DATA

Names: Cameron, John B., author.
Title: Tar Heels in gray : life in the 30th North Carolina infantry
    in the Civil War / John B. Cameron.
Other titles: Life in the 30th North Carolina infantry in the Civil War
Description: Jefferson, North Carolina : McFarland & Company, Inc.,
    Publishers, 2021 | Includes bibliographical references and index.
Identifiers: LCCN 2021039970 | ISBN 9781476683263
    (paperback : acid free paper) ∞
    ISBN 9781476643588 (ebook)
Subjects: LCSH: Confederate States of America. Army. North Carolina
    Infantry Regiment, 30th. Company H. | North Carolina—History—
    Civil War, 1861–1865—Regimental histories. | United States—History—
    Civil War, 1861–1865—Regimental histories. | United States—History—
    Civil War, 1861–1865—Campaigns. | BISAC: HISTORY / Military /
    United States | HISTORY / United States / Civil War Period (1850–1877)
Classification: LCC E573.5 30th .C36 2021 | DDC 973.7/456—dc23
LC record available at https://lccn.loc.gov/2021039970

BRITISH LIBRARY CATALOGUING DATA ARE AVAILABLE

ISBN (print) 978-1-4766-8326-3
ISBN (ebook) 978-1-4766-4358-8

On the cover *left to right:* brothers John and David Sloan, Company H,
30th North Carolina. David ended the war as a POW, and John died of
pneumonia in November 1862 (courtesy Mark Sloan).
Background: Split rail fence in autumn at Gettysburg National Military Park
in Gettysburg, Pennsylvania (© KateShort/Shutterstock)

Printed in the United States of America

McFarland & Company, Inc., Publishers
  Box 611, Jefferson, North Carolina 28640
  www.mcfarlandpub.com

To Abby

Acknowledgments

All writing, including that of history, is a solitary craft. However, behind that lone pen there often stands a crowd of people who made the writing possible.

History above all relies on data and documents. Over several decades it has been my privilege to work with archivists in several countries and states. In the writing of this book I am especially indebted to archivists at Perkins Library of Duke University who led me to several important collections, and to the archivists of the University of Notre Dame who provided me with digital copies of letters before they were available online.

Two people, Annie Thomas and Charlie Harrington (both of Broadway, North Carolina), were not archivists but should be called honorary archivists. They carefully preserved letters from the past and generously permitted me to copy them.

If archivists are the foundation of historical writing, the building of the edifice is made possible by the encouragement and support of individuals. More people than I have space to name contributed to making me a historian and to the writing of this book. I.J. Stephenson taught me to love learning and history when I was in high school. My mentor at Chapel Hill, George V. Taylor, molded me into a historian and taught me to write history. Daniel Honeycutt and the 30th N.C. Infantry reenactors encouraged me and provided me with copies of letters. No number of words would be sufficient to acknowledge the exceptional help of Robert Hirsh, MD. Dr. Hirsh put his encyclopedic knowledge of medicine and the history of medicine into the chapters on survival and disease. Without his participation neither of those chapters would have been possible. Finally my special thanks to my wife Abby, whose constant support and encouragement has made it possible for me to devote myself to writing.

Table of Contents

Preface

This book's very long gestation began when I was in high school and discovered letters from Civil War family members in a relative's trunk. I carefully transcribed the letters with no goal in mind. Word got out in my small town that I was interested in such things, and other people asked if I would like to read letters they had. Letters were photocopied or transcribed and filed away.

I attended college and graduate school where I studied French history. The Civil War was far from my mind. I moved about from state to state, dragging the folders of letters with me. Somehow they survived through dozens of moves, neglected for many years.

A few years ago I opened up the folders and started reading. The letters were intriguing, and the largest number was from two men in the same regiment and company—Company H of the 30th North Carolina Infantry. The regiment was involved in most of the major battles in Virginia from the Seven Days through the surrender at Appomattox. As I looked deeper, I found more and more letters and diaries from other men in the same regiment in archives. The men's stories and their fates fascinated me.

Actual battles were distinctly of secondary interest to me. Moreover, the military history of the 30th North Carolina had been adequately discussed twice, first by Michael Taylor, *To Drive the Enemy from Southern Soil*, and second by William Venner, *The 30th North Carolina Infantry in the Civil War.* What kept pulling me were the men themselves. Gradually some important questions about them began to coalesce.

The first question was how could these men, most of whom were not owners of enslaved people, be induced to fight and die to defend the terrible institution of slavery? The second question grew out of the fact that the men were so poorly fed and clothed that many of them deserted. Given that, why did any of these men stay in the field and continue to fight? It is clear that even many of those who stayed considered desertion as their best choice.

The goal of this book is to answer not just the two questions posed above about the men but others as well. What was their economic status? To what extent were they involved in the institution of slavery? What were their lives like in the army? What were their hardships and fleeting joys? What diseases affected them and, in many cases, killed them? Why did they believe they were fighting and did those views change over time? In short, we seek an in-depth description of the men themselves, not their battles.

Certainly the true underlying cause of the war was to preserve slavery. The call to arms by those in power in North Carolina—themselves apparently quite willing to destroy the Union to preserve slavery—was not, however, presented that way to the average man. The appeal for volunteers played on the ingrained love of what men imagined war to be. It was presented as a war to defend family, state and honor. Letters reveal that initially many men, rich and poor, embraced that war with enthusiasm.

When the volunteers faced the reality of war, and they did so quickly—that there was little or no glory and a great deal of horror and death—they were by then committed and most were reluctant to change course.

The contemporary historiography of the Civil War has begun to move away from pure battle history and toward social and economic analyses. Recent studies of the Army of North Virginia have sought to describe the social status and the motivation of soldiers by using samples. To date, sampling has been the only reasonable approach, for there are too few detailed regimental studies to enable a compiled study of states or armies as a whole. Other broad studies have dealt with motivation and the question of class divisions in the antebellum South. This book is very much of that same approach.

Many of my conclusions about the 30th North Carolina—social status, ownership of slaves, presence of free men of color, motivation—differ sharply from some studies of larger units based on small samples. I do not claim that my findings are necessarily more representative of the whole than analyses based on samples. I hope that this description of the 30th North Carolina will be joined by other regimental studies based on extensive research rather than samples. Only when many such monographs are available can a future historian describe the social/economic reality of an entire state, the Army of Northern Virginia or the Confederate Army as a whole.

I have sought to write the history of the men of the 30th North Carolina as they were. Soldiers in time of war are motivated to fight, kill and die for many reasons. We need to understand even those whom we now see as deeply flawed or tragically mistaken in their willingness to defend the indefensible.

The men of the 30th North Carolina Infantry paid a terrible price for waging their war. It is not simply that they deserve to be understood, but that we ourselves need to understand them. In a real sense they represent all soldiers (people), North and South, black and white, our fathers, our brothers, our sons and now our daughters.

Introduction

In 1860, a small but influential number of wealthy North Carolinians were determined to preserve slavery by taking their state out of the Union so it could join the Confederacy being formed by the states of the lower South. If that involved war, it bothered them not at all. They believed any war would be over in a matter of weeks with little bloodshed. Their tactics were at first simple and straightforward.

In early 1861, the state legislature, controlled by the well-to-do, authorized a public vote to be held on 28 February 1861, on whether to call a constitutional convention that would carry out secession.[1] Counties with a large enslaved population like New Hanover on the coast and Mecklenburg further west voted heavily in favor of the convention. In counties where slave owning was much smaller, the vote was overwhelmingly not to call the convention. Consider the vote in Moore County in the center of the state, whose population was largely small to middling farmers, most of whom owned no slaves—1,257 no and only 135 yes. The statewide vote was narrowly against: 46,672 yes and 47,323 no. The vote may well have reflected stronger opposition to secession than the numbers imply for some influential people opposed to secession had campaigned in favor of calling the convention. They believed that the men elected to the convention could be convinced to vote against secession and thereby settle the question permanently.

The secessionist party reached its nadir in early March when Lincoln's inaugural address seemed to be conciliatory to the South and when the peace delegates sent from North Carolina and Virginia to meet with Lincoln seemed to be having some success. Then came the assault on Fort Sumter in April 1861. That attack turned what had been a peaceful dissolving of the Union, which most Americans thought perfectly legal, into an illegal rebellion and state of war. President

Lincoln now had a legal, constitutional right—perhaps even duty—to put down the rebellion. He therefore called for 75,000 volunteers to defeat rebellion. North Carolina secessionists were re-energized.

The final campaign for secession, supported by propaganda, was tightly controlled by the pro-secessionists. War was portrayed as inevitable. It would be short and relatively bloodless, but North Carolina could not avoid fighting. The only choice was, so said the secessionists, to fight on the side of our cousins and relatives in the rest of the South or war against our own families. This was, in truth, not purely rhetorical. During the early 19th century thousands of people from North Carolina had migrated south into the states on the Gulf of Mexico, including Texas. Some influential men who had been staunch unionists, citing reluctance to war against cousins, began to favor secession. As Zebulon Vance—who would be governor during the war and United States senator afterwards—recalled later, he was speaking against secession with his hand raised making a gesture when he heard of Lincoln's call for troops. He said, "When my hand came down from that impassioned gesticulation, it fell slowly and sadly by the side of a secessionist." Could North Carolina have stayed in the Union and refused to send troops? The question is unanswerable since no such attempt was made.

Building on the idea that war was inevitable, Governor Ellis and the secessionists put into place a well-thought-out and highly un-democratic plan to achieve victory. The legislature for the second time authorized a convention to meet on 20 May 1861. This time there would be no popular vote on whether or not to hold the convention, only an election of its members. The delegates chosen were decidedly from the upper economic levels of society and, therefore, skewed heavily toward defense of slavery. This was hardly an aberration. Most political offices were held by well-to-do men. Very few poor men could afford to run for office and if they ran, even fewer could afford to serve what were practically unpaid positions. Only 27 percent of North Carolina free families owned slaves and 67 percent of those owned fewer than 10 slaves. The average slave owner in North Carolina owned fewer than 10 slaves.[2] By comparison the convention delegates were far richer—the average number of slaves owned per delegate was 30.5 and the mean number of slaves owned was 21. Average real estate and personal property of the delegates was $61,817, an enormous sum in

Introduction

1861. After several different resolutions were considered, the convention voted unanimously to leave the Union.

Governor Ellis, understanding the possibility of continued opposition to secession in the state, persuaded the convention not to submit the resolution to a popular referendum. Upon the adjournment of the convention, North Carolina was no longer a member of the United States. The governor asked at once that the state be admitted into the Confederacy and that government acquiesced.

In order to ensure that the decision could not be reconsidered, Governor Ellis gave orders to seize all federal property in the state, thereby putting North Carolina into a state of rebellion and war against the Union. Ellis never knew the tragedy that would result from his actions. He died in office in the summer of 1861. The secessionists had won. By the fall of 1861, the Union was making plans to occupy much of eastern North Carolina and to blockade all shipping in and out of the state as a part of putting down its rebellion.

The men who had so foolishly taken North Carolina into rebellion were now faced with defending the state against a well-armed, well-trained army. The occupation of eastern North Carolina by Union forces was, of course, portrayed as an invasion. North Carolina had few military resources and only a scant militia made up of untrained, often older men. In near panic, the legislature called for volunteers to form companies and regiments in a North Carolina army for a term of 12 months. Each man would be given a $50 bounty and a monthly wage. From July through September of 1861, men met and volunteered in large numbers all over North Carolina.

The motivation for these volunteers was not state's rights, to preserve slavery or defend the South. The recruiting propaganda stressed that any decent, God-fearing man would volunteer to defend his family, especially his women, against the brutal robbers, rapists and murderers who would soon be arriving. The fight would be short, exciting and heroic. Those same men, who voted to preserve the Union in February of 1861, six months later were motivated to wage war against it.

In Moore County, where so many had voted against secession, 80 men, joined by 12 from neighboring Chatham County, signed on and formed a company. Moore County had already formed one infantry company, Company H of the 26th North Carolina, and in November 1861 would form Company C of the 35th North Carolina as well as a company in the 2nd North Carolina Cavalry. In 1862 yet another company was formed, Company F of the 50th North Carolina. In all, Moore County would see 1,500 men inducted, not always willingly, into Confederate service. This was more than voted against secession in 1860 and virtually all the young free males in the county.[3]

This book is about the fate of the 92 men who volunteered in Moore County in August 1861 and 1,400 others who were joined with them to form a regiment—the 30th North Carolina—that principal unit of Civil War battle. Over the course of three and one-half years, 1,506 men—approximately 1,000 volunteers and 500 drafted and often forced into the army against their wishes—would be a part of the 30th North Carolina Infantry Regiment. The regiment would find itself center stage for many of the decisive events of the Civil War. In June 1862, it was assigned to what would become the Army of Northern Virginia. It would fight under D.H. Hill, Thomas Jackson, Jubal Early and Robert E. Lee in nearly all the major battles of that army, surrendering at Appomattox. Three times it crossed the Potomac into Union territory—twice as part of the lead battalion. Twice it penetrated deeper into the North than any other unit. It was the rear guard retreating from Gettysburg, and it probably fired the last shots from the Army of Northern Virginia in April 1865. We will give a summary military history of the regiment, where it went, where it fought. However, battle is not our focus. Rather, our interest is the soldiers themselves. It is the tragic story of men, the majority poor, who were maneuvered into fighting and dying in an attempt to preserve the interests of rich men who often avoided the war themselves.

Drawing on the large number of letters, diaries, memoirs and other personal documents from and to the men of the 30th North Carolina, I intend to describe what day-to-day life was like. Why did they volunteer? How did they live and die? How could men so independent and untrained become such hardened soldiers? What were the fleeting pleasures of camp life? Why did so many die of dysentery, typhoid and infection? Why did so many desert while so many others fought to the hopeless end? Well before the end of the war many of the survivors were disillusioned and had come to realize that they had been tricked into being part of a "Big Man's war fought by Little Men" even as they continued to fight.

1

Confusion Was
the Order of the Day

"My feet is so sore that I cant hardly walk."
—Louis McLeod

On 11 September 1861, 92 men assembled in eastern Moore County, North Carolina, to pursue what they had been assured would be a short adventure to drive back an expected invasion of the North Carolina coast. They had been promised, but not yet paid, a $50 bounty and a small wage for the 12-month enlistment that would be necessary to keep North Carolina free and force the United States to call off the invasion. The men had already chosen company officers and non-commissioned officers when they gathered at Swann Station on the eastern side of the county.

There were two good reasons to meet at Swann Station. First, the company had elected a young member of the prominent Swann family as its captain.[1] Second, there was a railroad being constructed to link Fayetteville with Chatham County, and it had already reached the Swann plantation.[2] The interior transportation available in Moore County in 1861 was limited to stagecoach lines which ran from Carthage, the county seat, in several directions along dirt roads which dated to the 18th century and which followed older Indian and game paths. Because the men were going to Wilmington to be sworn in as North Carolina soldiers, they could travel in comfort by rail to Fayetteville and then by river boat down the Cape Fear River.

The major cities of North Carolina—Charlotte, Raleigh, Wilmington, Weldon, New Bern and Goldsboro—were already linked by rail and tied into the Petersburg, Virginia Railroad. In 1858, a new rail line,

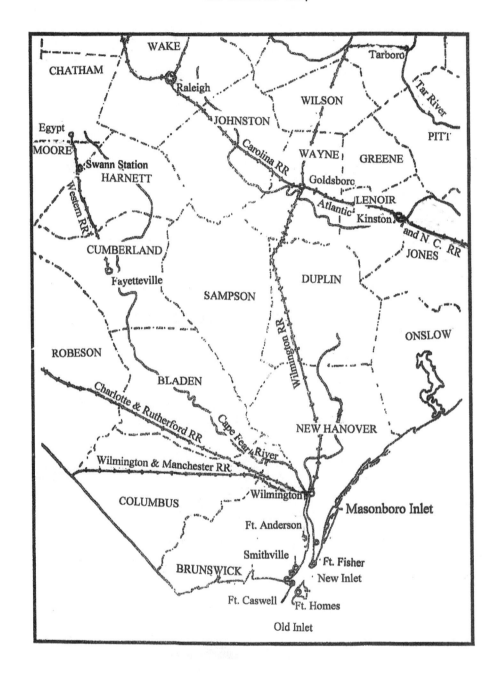

Figure 1. Eastern North Carolina in 1861

the Western Railroad, began construction. It would link Fayetteville and the Cape Fear River with the Deep River coal fields in Chatham County.[3] Some coal had been dug in southern Chatham County since the 18th century, but in the 1850s a major effort was made by sinking what came to be known as the Egypt coal mine. This mine was the main source of coal in North Carolina and transporting the coal to Fayetteville for use in river and coastal steamers was seen as potentially very profitable. By 1860, the Western Railroad reached from Fayetteville to the edge of Moore County where it crossed the Swann plantation. By the fall of 1861, the line reached Rollins Store (soon to be called Jonesboro) in the northeast part of Moore County that 50 years later would be organized as a new county. Lee County was named for the man who oversaw the deaths of hundreds of the young men who enlisted. Early in 1863, the Western was completed to Egypt and from that time on coal was shipped down to Fayetteville with ease.[4]

The trip from Swann Station to Fayetteville was quick and easy and must have been quite an adventure for men who had never been on a train or river boat before.[5] In Fayetteville they moved from rail head to the Cape Fear docks and boarded a river boat for Wilmington which they reached on the 12th after traveling all night. It turned out, however, that they had either been misinformed, or more likely given no directions at all from state officials. The Wilmington authorities advised company officers that they were supposed to be in Raleigh, not Wilmington. In order to reach Raleigh they needed to travel to Goldsboro, so they climbed aboard a train and after a second all-night trip arrived at Goldsboro at 10 a.m. on the 13th. At 4 that afternoon they left Goldsboro on a second train for Raleigh and after a third overnight ride were in the capital by 9 a.m. on the 14th. They were quickly marched to Rock Church where they slept that night and then on the 15th marched to Camp Mangum.[6] With proper instructions they could, of course, have easily walked to Raleigh on the 11th.

The men would spend two weeks in Raleigh, becoming acquainted with military routine, and be accepted as an official North Carolina unit. It had been a long, confused trip with a lot of walking. One of the men who made the trip was Louis McLeod.[7] We will cite McLeod often during our discussion of 1861–1862. He and his wife Eliza wrote frequently to each other and many of the letters from each have survived. The McLeod letters read like hearing a conversation—observations on many aspects of life, problems each faced and both praise and criticism of their lives apart. They make up a remarkable source for the camp life of the 30th North Carolina.

Upon arriving in Raleigh, McLeod wrote to his wife on 16 September that his feet were so sore that he could hardly walk. Three other companies were at the camp and when two more came, they formed a regiment. Within a few weeks nine companies recruited from other counties would be joined with the men from Moore County making the 30th Infantry Regiment of North Carolina.

The Moore County company was named Company H. Company A[8] was raised in Sampson County, Company B in Warren County, Company C in Brunswick County, Company D in Wake and Granville Counties, Company E in Duplin County, Company F in Edgecombe County, Company G in Granville County, Company I in Nash County, and Company K in Mecklenburg County.

It is doubtful that the men at Camp Mangum received much training but at least the company officers—a captain, lieutenants, sergeants and corporals—were confirmed and they were mustered into state service. In addition the men received uniforms of some sort. Louis McLeod, who was elected corporal in Company H, wrote his wife that he was some boy, with a new suit of clothes and a new cap. He felt "big." Also, his feet were now well.

On Saturday, 28 September, the men of the newly named 30th North Carolina left Raleigh to go back to Wilmington. The fact that they were now an official unit with proper orders did not ensure a pleasant and easy trip. First, they traveled in box cars rather than passenger coaches. To make it even worse the box cars had recently hauled horses and apparently were barely mucked out, much less cleaned. Second, no provision was made for food on the trip, and the train didn't pause at all along the way. When the hungry men arrived in Wilmington not enough food had been prepared, so quite a few had to buy breakfast on their own. It is likely that many of them had no money at all and must have gone hungry. After breakfast, the men were put in a warehouse with guards to keep them from straying.

The next morning, the 29th, they marched a mile to Camp Wyatt,[9] put up tents and made camp. They were soon joined by another regiment of 1,150 men. Serious training could not be undertaken, however, because neither regiment had any weapons and the 30th was not fully organized—it had no commander.

The adventure for the volunteers was barely two weeks old and was proving to be a trip down a much rougher road than anticipated. In addition to lack of food, filthy and smelly transportation and a great deal of walking, the men encountered many other problems. Corporal McLeod had left home with $3.25 plus some paper money which he put into a newly purchased little purse. Somehow in the confusion he lost the purse, or it was stolen, and so he had survived in the Raleigh camp with only $2.85. In 1860 Moore County, like most of rural North Carolina, there was very little specie in circulation. The economy was mostly barter. When supplies such as salt or tools were needed, it was necessary to travel to Fayetteville, sell oats, wheat, cotton or some other crop to get money with which to purchase what was needed.[10] Corporal McLeod had nothing to barter, and he must have had a very difficult time without money.

From the beginning men made the usual complaints about military life and food. The victuals served in the camp at Wilmington had many officers grumbling, but McLeod thought they were not bad. He reported that they had plenty of everything except molasses—that staple of every meal—of which they had none. On the other hand patriotic spirits in camp were boosted by a "splendid" show put on by Captain Duncan Moore's Artillery Company.[11] Horses were racing and running, cannon unlimbered and mock fired, all to the excitement of the men.

The massive confusion was intensified from the beginning by a staggering amount of disease. With close to 2,000 men on one field close to each other and without adequate sanitation, few remained healthy. These rural men had led fairly isolated lives before 1861 and as a result had little immunity to infectious disease. Diseases spread rapidly through camps especially measles, mumps and "hooping" cough. There was so much coughing that McLeod said he never slept at all one night. By the time the 30th was installed in its temporary bivouac at Camp Wyatt three men had already died.[12]

2

A Fully Formed Regiment

*"I committed a great mistake in not joining the Regt.
Sooner after I was elected; they have gone on so long
without any directing head, that they think they are
nearly free."*
　　　　　　　　　　　—Francis Parker, October 1861

Confederate regiments were created nearly *sui generis*. When
North Carolina began to raise regiments in the fall of 1861, it did so
with little guidance. Certainly the authorities had recourse, as did all
states, to manuals published by the United States Army, manuals that
provided a structure and Table of Organization. They also relied when
they could on former United States Army personnel. Future Confederate Lieutenant General D.H. Hill was responsible for much of the
early planning in North Carolina.[1] In 1860, he left his professorship
at Davidson College and became commandant of the North Carolina
Military Academy in Charlotte. In 1861, he was brought to Raleigh
with the rank of colonel to organize North Carolina's volunteers at
Camp Mangum. By the summer, he was commander of the 1st North
Carolina Regiment which went to Virginia in response to the landing
of Union troops. By May 1862, he had been promoted to major general and was commanding a division under Joseph Johnston in eastern
Virginia. North Carolina had very few men with such military experience and skill.

The 30th, so far as can be determined, had no veterans of the
Mexican War or former United States Army personnel.[2] Practically
everything had to be created and accomplished by men who had little
or no direct knowledge of military matters or organization.

The tasks facing the officers of the 30th were herculean. Men had
to be turned into soldiers by men who were not themselves soldiers;

personnel had to be clothed, fed and housed; the large number of men living in close proximity necessitated sanitary facilities though such efforts were seldom sufficient to prevent disease. All armies insist on voluminous records being kept, and the infant army was no different. Most records have not survived to the present but it is clear that from 1861 to 1863 an attempt was made to keep accurate company and regimental records. Because the regiment was the basic unit designed to operate on its own, supplies and transportation had to be provided for provisions and for movement in the field.

The 30th North Carolina may have arrived at Camp Wyatt ready for work but no real training could take place until the regiment was fully formed. According to the authorization for volunteer units, the company-grade officers were to meet and elect regimental officers. Before leaving Raleigh, company officers had chosen a lieutenant colonel, Draughan,[3] a major, James T. Kell,[4] and a chaplain.[5] Their choice for colonel, however, did not accept and without a colonel the regiment lacked real direction. Companies were drilling and training as best they could but discipline was exceedingly lax, and one suspects that little was accomplished. John W. Bone of Company I remembered several decades later that when they arrived his company at least was mostly drunk and ready to fight each other if no Yankees were available. Those who were sober became guards to keep the drunks together.[6] Whiskey would prove to be a long-lasting and serious problem for the commanders. For nearly all of October, the regiment floundered without a commander.

The second man offered the colonelcy, and the man who put an end to much of the confusion, was Francis Marion "Frank" Parker.[7] By all accounts the men were fortunate in their choice. Parker, a wealthy planter, had been quick to volunteer for the 1st North Carolina. When he was offered command of the 30th North Carolina, Parker was still serving in the 1st North Carolina with the rank of captain. He had seen combat at Big Bethel under Colonel D.H. Hill and was a man determined to train the men and see that they were led in the best possible way. He wrote his wife on 26 October that he had arrived and was pleased with the camp and the other officers. Two of the captains were "old" men of near 50 and he did feel odd giving them orders. By the 29th he had achieved an understanding of his men. He thought the regiment was made up of good men but it was, however, in great confusion. Parker regretted that he had not come at once on being elected instead of waiting. The men "have gone on so long without any directing head, that they think they are nearly free."[8]

There were two large problems that confronted Colonel Parker as he began the training of his regiment. First, after 45 days with no commander the men did see themselves as free. They had no understanding of military discipline and little or no desire to make its acquaintance.[9] They were far more interested in getting whiskey and slipping into Wilmington. Second, they had no weapons.

When the war began, North Carolina did not have a large stock of muskets and other weapons. To make matters worse, much of what was in storage had been sent to Virginia in an early act of solidarity to resist the Union invasion. Now North Carolina needed those weapons but had no success in convincing Virginia to return them. The situation was so dire that Robert E. Lee—serving in planning and supply, not yet in command—seriously suggested to state authorities that only center-line companies be issued muskets. The others should be given pikes with which they could defend themselves.[10] It was not until well into 1862 that the problem was partially solved by enlarging the former Federal Armory at Fayetteville with machinery and rifle works from the captured Federal Arsenal at Harpers Ferry.[11]

Military activity in camp consisted of picket duty to guard against surprise attack by the enemy and guard duty to keep your own men in line and away from supplies. Training in the 19th century consisted of endless repetition of two series of movements: loading and firing; marching and deploying. Certainly there were few Americans in 1860 who did not know guns and how to load and fire them. The great majority were rural men and probably most were hunters. However, the military did things differently. The objective was to deliver a concentrated barrage of fire on the enemy which meant loading and firing *en masse* and doing so while moving and under fire yourself. Tearing a paper cartridge with the teeth, pouring and packing powder, shot and wadding, proper use of flints or caps, aiming and firing, all these actions had to be mastered until the soldier did them quickly, coolly and without much thought.[12]

In the 1850s, United States Secretary of War Jefferson Davis had begun to upgrade the weapons in the U.S. Army to quick-loading rifles that had more accuracy and longer range. In 1861, state militias still used muzzle loaders. The new weapons purchased by Davis should have led to new battlefield tactics but no changes had been made by 1861. West Point continued to teach tactics throughout the 1850s that had been developed by Napoleon in order to concentrate fire from weapons not accurate over 50 yards. The tactics necessitated moving men in columns as quickly and efficiently as possible to the edge of the battlefield and then to form a line of battle with the utmost speed and minimum confusion. That is, to change from a column to a wide attack formation. Thus, each company knew its place in column and regimental line of battle.[13] Any time the regiment was not marching it was drilling. There were often new men to bring up to the proficiency of the old timers, and the movements like loading and firing, done to the beat of drums, had to be instinctive.[14]

Once weapons were secured and training begun, camp life for the 30th found the military routines of rise, eat, march, practice and sleep, all marked by the roll of the drum. Yet, men are not robots. We resist such regimentation and find ways even in a military camp to continue what we value in life. Friends and enemies are made. Men, especially on Sunday, seized time to relax and for pleasure.

3

The Pretend War

Life in Camp

The North Carolina General Assembly authorized the formation of state militia companies and then volunteer companies and regiments for defense in the Second Special Session of 1861.[1] In order to maximize time for training, much of the construction and non-military work was to be done by civilians. Each company was authorized to enroll up to four cooks who would be rationed and paid by the state and up to four laundresses to be rationed by the state at the same rate as men, but paid by the men of the company for whom they washed.[2] The actual numbers enrolled in the 30th varied from company to company. Requisitions for food supplies from September 1861 give the number of men and women present in companies.[3] Company B had only one "laundress" while Company E had four. Similarly the number of civilian men enrolled also varied from company to company.

Free men of color were not supposed to be enrolled as soldiers though, as we will show below, some were. However, authorizing legislation specifically said free men of color could be employed as civilian workers.[4] Such men were clearly hired at wages to do work and were in no sense enrolled in the army.[5] At least two free men of color from Moore County, Hardy Harris[6] and Ingram Bass, were employed by Company H. They seem to have been tempted to slip away to Wilmington rather than work. In his letter of 23 February 1862, Louis McLeod wrote that Captain Swann had gone on horseback to Wilmington to find the two men and bring them back to camp.[7] In addition, several of the well-to-do officers brought one or two body servants, or slaves, with them. Were these men fed by the company or were they fed from the private stores of the officer? We do not know precisely though John Witherspoon[8] returned from furlough in late September 1861 with two "Negro boys" and he drew three days' rations for them.[9] Requisition forms simply listed number of men and number of women who drew rations with no other description.

Whatever the numbers of men, and women, present in each company, they had to be fed. In September 1861, food seems to have been at least adequate. Louis McLeod remarked often to his wife that he thought so. Some officers grumbled the fare was not good enough, but McLeod thought it was fine and of sufficient quantity. For example, for the four days of 7–10 September 1861, Company B requisitioned rations for 57 men and one woman and Company E for 73 men and four women. For Company E this meant four days' rations for 77 persons, a total of 308 rations. The requisition lists number of rations rather than pounds or other measurements: fresh beef 154; pork 124; flour 211; no beans; rice, coffee, sugar, vinegar, candles, soap, salt 308 each; meal 77; molasses 308.[10] The quality may not have been the best, but there must have been sufficient food available.

The regiment continued to equip its men with more comfort and military accouterments through the rest of 1861. On 19 November 1861, Captain Joseph Green[11] of Company C signed for 80 blankets, 62 canteens, six canteen straps, 38 pairs of shoes, 56 caps, two officers' tents, three axes, one hatchet, 20 bed sacks.[12]

Keeping records required paper and nearly all officers in the 30th requisitioned paper, ink and writing implements. For example, in the fourth quarter of 1862 Quartermaster Buckner Williams required three quires of letter paper and one bottle of ink.[13]

Amusements in Camp

> "We have a heep of fun & a heep of hard times"
> —A. F. Harrington

Despite sickness and hard drill, the men stole time for excitement and fun. As long as they were in North Carolina they found many ways to amuse themselves. There were some musical instruments in camp. Colonel Parker wrote to his wife more than once that he could hear banjo and fiddle as he wrote. This must have been a normal part of camp life. Letters, however, written home by ordinary soldiers do not mention music. Perhaps so commonplace it did not seem worth mentioning, or perhaps Parker was embellishing the truth to comfort his wife.

Officers raced their horses. One would assume that in cavalry units such events would have been common but in the infantry only officers had horses. Pvt. Ardrey noted in his diary on 16 April 1862 that Major Kell's horse lost in a race to that of Williams.[14]

Some of the amusements, while natural for country men, show considerable laxness in the camp especially late in the spring of 1862. A.F. Harrington[15] wrote to his nephew J.K.P. Harrington[16] in April 1862, "We have hounds down here too, a good pack."[17] He described a hunt with them that very morning in which they caught a wild cat. The day before, he had gone fishing. "Plenty of game here," he reported. Many letters mention catching fish and oysters to eat which was preferable to the often-inferior food served in the messes.

What seems to have been most desired, if one had any money, was getting a day or two to go to Wilmington.[18] There you could have a great meal at Bishop's Hotel. Louis McLeod was effusive in describing one such: "They had fresh pork and chicken meete and greans and twenips and peas and beats squashed irish potatoes new and sweete potatoes and everry thing that was good and you better believ I set to it like a bline kitten to a pan of nails. I eat there every time I go to Wilmington but I have to pay seventy five cents for it. It seams verry high but the dinner is verry good and money plenty as the old saying."[19]

In Wilmington, you could have your picture taken by a photographer, get whiskey and doubtless engage in other activities that were not written about to wives and mothers. It is highly likely that with so many soldiers nearby, the number of prostitutes in Wilmington increased proportionally. Of course, few men would mention this in letters home to wives, mothers and fathers. Nor did Ardrey mention the topic in his diary. He did, however, note quite a few trips to Wilmington. One exception was John Witherspoon who teased his wife in a letter by saying, "I am all alone. I could get plenty of company if I would only say so but, I might possibly get some disease."[20] Louis McLeod told his wife that her nephew Tan[21] had "been to town" and was very sick as a result, meaning that he had drunk a lot of whiskey.

William Ardrey noted in his diary on 5 April 1862 that he had been to Wilmington and had his picture taken. Louis McLeod asked his wife to send the "likenesses" that they had of each other to him and he would have a man from Wilmington create a large image of them together. She did so but with great fear that the pictures, still a very rare thing in 1862, would be lost. No further mention was made of the pictures, so we don't know if her fears were realized. There were also photographers who traveled out to the camp to make pictures of individuals and even of entire companies. Company H had one such image made, and McLeod proudly sent it home to his family. However, his wife wrote him that the picture was so bad that neither she nor the children could recognize any of the men in it including him. Unfortunately all such pictures seem to have been lost or destroyed.

Proper young women from Wilmington or other nearby places often visited the camp on Sundays. These outings, much like Sunday afternoon picnics, always boosted the morale of the men who commented in letters and diaries about the pleasure they brought. In a similar fashion, there were friends and family from home bringing food, clothes and letters.[22]

Even later in 1863 the men continued to find ways to escape the war's horrors and provide some amusements. Rufus D. Stallings[23] wrote to the woman he hoped to marry someday about how the men filled up free time in camp. She had apparently asked him to tell her what they did. "Some of them is reading their testements. Some of them playing with the ball and the most of it all some of them is playing cards."[24] Were they playing baseball or some other form of ball? We can't know.[25]

As one might expect with so many young men in one place, there were often tricks and silliness in the air. Several men in Company H, growing tired of how much James Deaton[26] complained of being homesick and getting no letters, wrote one up and gave it to him.[27] When he realized it was a trick he stopped complaining. Ardrey noted that on 1 April 1862 he fooled some people and that on 2 May he "stole 2 chickens." He was also pleased that he found some local scuppernong wine on two occasions.

Friendship and Betrayal

"He is more than a brother to me."—Louis McLeod

Military life and training often forges very deep friendships. Such would seem to have been the case with Louis McLeod and Francis Moore.[28] McLeod mentions Moore first in his letter of 5 October when he comments that the company mess had no molasses at all. He, however, had some that day for he ate dinner with Lieutenant Moore and shared his private stock. The following Sunday, Moore invited McLeod to his father's nearby home and they stayed until Monday evening when they returned to camp. McLeod enjoyed himself "first rate." He thought, "Francis is one of the best fellers in the world. He is the best officer we have got."[29] The first third of the letter written on 30 October is all about Moore. Because McLeod had had most of his money stolen and they had not yet been paid, his friends, including Moore, loaned him some. Moore gave him room in his personal tent. Moore had a little stove in the tent which kept it warm, and he had his own cooking utensils. Francis "sayed it was no use of talking. I had to stay in the tent with him and lie by the stove where we could keep warm." McLeod was sending to Wilmington to get a cot and mattress even though it would cost $7 or $8 but that was not too much to spend for comfort during the winter. He asked Eliza to make him a new sack, or comforter, and stuff it with plenty of cotton. He was eating well with Francis. They cooked oysters on 29 October and "faired first rate. I never will perish a long as I am with him. I will stick to him as long as I can stick to my self. We are together all the time." By 3 November, McLeod had his "Beauregard camp cot" and had moved into the tent with Francis "where we have a nice little stove where he lies on one side of the stove and me on the other."

On 17 November, McLeod reported that he had been very sick with "the big measles and Francis was taken to bed sick last Sunday, 10 November, with bilious fever." Moore was still sick on Friday and left to go home near Wilmington to recuperate. "I was never so sorry to see a man leave me in my life. Ah, my wife, he is more than a brother ever was to me. He told me when he left me lying on the bed that if I did get bad off he would send for me as soon as his father came down and take me over to his place where the greatest attention would be given me."

On 2 December, McLeod wrote that Moore was very sick and still away. "I miss him so much. I had rather any body else was sick than him. We were together all of the time when he was here. And if we ever got into a fight we will be together. We had done made up our minds to fight side by side. If one got shot down the other was to shoot down the man that done it or die in the attempt. I wish he was well and back here now."

In late January, Moore was still not back with the unit but perhaps not because of sickness. McLeod wrote on 26 January, "If Francis Moore is up there [in Chatham County] you can send [coffee] by him and ... send me any thing else you wish and have to spair and if Francis is up there I want you to tell him I want him to come home very bad. I don't know what to do about moving until he comes back. I am afraid I will bee cut out of a room with him."

On 1 February 1862, Eliza gave birth to her last child named Francis Moore Parker McLeod. But little more would be said about Moore. On 13 February, he resigned from the company by reason of "pulmonary consumption." His resignation was accepted about 27 February. It is, of course, very possible that Lieutenant Moore truly was suffering from tuberculosis. However, I think it more likely that his very wealthy father persuaded him to take that way out of the army and danger. Moore wrote Captain Swann that his life would be endangered by further duty and this was the opinion of his family physician.[30] The fact that Louis McLeod ceased to refer to him after he left the army makes that possibility even more likely. When McLeod referred to his son in the spring of 1862, he always referred to him as Parker never as Francis.

What seemed to have begun as an exceptionally close bond of two men, almost as brothers, must have ended with anger and a sense of betrayal. Though Francis Moore may have been sick in the winter of 1861–1862, it was far from fatal. It can't be certain how he spent the rest of the war years, but on 11 May 1862 Eliza McLeod wrote to Louis, "Frances more [sic] is up her now and his father too[.] Tha brot thirty or forty negros up her." Moore was certainly healthy enough to be working, alongside his father, a large gang of enslaved men. Much later on 11 March 1895, he married a young woman named Mary Groves.

Francis Marsden Moore survived as a prosperous farmer with several children until he died on 3 March 1911, nearly 50 years after the death of his "brother" Louis McLeod.

The Water of Life

"We cant live here without a little whisky to mix with our watter."
—Louis McLeod

In 1860s North Carolina, many people viewed whiskey as an essential ingredient of life. Rich and poor, men and women, all saw whiskey as necessary to hold off disease and to live a normal life. The early letters from both McLeod and his wife Eliza are filled with complaints that whiskey is now so expensive that they can afford little or none. Whiskey was readily available; peddlers were on the edges of the camp but the men, not having been paid since enlisting, had no money.

Colonel Parker gave strict orders against any whiskey in the camp and even arrested a few whiskey sellers from Wilmington who came to the camp. When the colonel's wife sent him some whiskey to mix with his water he asked her not to do so again. He thanked her but told her that he had forbidden all whiskey in camp and he should set the example.

References to whiskey-drinking in letters would indicate it was not a genteel activity, at least not for men. Men often drank until they were dead drunk, bringing on one or more days of severe hangover and sickness. In Raleigh during the organization of the regiment, McLeod related that D.P. Morris[31] got "a little foxy" and was very sick. Tandy Walker went to town and was sick as could be. John Walker[32] wrote to McLeod that he had "taken on too much steam" and for two days was very sick but he recovered. From home, Abel Douglass[33] wrote that he had gone "on a tear" thinking it would cure his cold. It did not and in fact had made him so sick that he could barely function for two days. J.W. Bone in his memoir written late in life remembered that when his company arrived on the coast from Raleigh many were drinking and fighting each other since there were no Yankees to fight. McLeod didn't mention the drinking and fighting but wrote his wife that many

24

of the men had to be locked into a warehouse to keep them under control.[34]

It is clear that Colonel Parker was wise to keep whiskey far away from his men. But it would seep in. James Mashburn[35] of Company H managed to get enough to fill up his canteen before he went on guard duty in early January 1862. When the canteen was empty he fired off his rifle into the air twice and was so drunk that he was arrested, court-martialed and sentenced to 10 days hard labor wearing a ball and chain of 15 pounds.[36]

Profiteering

> *"I have to tell you about the speculation chickens."*
> —Louis McLeod

War imposes great sacrifices, not all of which are voluntary. For those so inclined and willing to seize opportunities, it can also provide great opportunities and profit. The Continental Army hungered in the midst of plenty because Valley Forge farmers preferred to sell their produce at high prices to the occupying British in Philadelphia. Historians long ago demolished the myth of the "lost cause" in which every Southerner bravely gave all he had to the cause of Confederate independence only to be overwhelmed by numerous and cruel occupiers. It should, therefore, come of little surprise to readers of this book that many men sought to profit from the war.

The earliest indication, as in most other wars, was that prices quickly began to rise on all things. This was most difficult for ordinary people because the amount of specie in circulation was small. Inflation was further exacerbated by the uncertainty of Confederate victory and, therefore, the dubious value of Confederate money. Major Sillers[37] advised his sister to settle his debts with Confederate money if she could, but warned that many would not take it since it was "not legal tender."[38]

Merchants everywhere increased prices. Those who sold items desirable to soldiers, especially whiskey and tobacco, swarmed around the encampments. Even when Colonel Parker, having forbidden whiskey in the camp, began to arrest men who came to sell it, the supply kept up even though the price reached the astronomical level of $.75 a quart. Louis McLeod complained to his wife that when they arrived at Wilmington it had been as high as $.50 but soon was at least $.75. The men couldn't buy it at that price.

One popular image of the Civil War has long been that every Rebel soldier carried tobacco and every Union soldier coffee and that in lulls of fighting they exchanged these things. Perhaps it was true on occasion, but the men of the 30th North Carolina in the fall of 1861 had no tobacco.[39] McLeod commented that he had never heard such grumbling about shortages. It wasn't that no tobacco was available. Plenty could be purchased all around the camp if a man had money. In late October, two months after mustering in, the men still had not been paid; only the wealthy had any money. McLeod expected they would all hurry and buy tobacco as soon as they were paid.

Pay day finally arrived on 31 October 1861. Monthly pay was computed for captains at $130, 1st lieutenants at $90, 2nd lieutenants at $80, and 3rd lieutenants at $60. Enlisted men drew far less: sergeants $17, corporals $13, musicians $12 and privates $11. Later there would be supplemental pay for some: teamsters, ambulance drivers and pioneers received $.25 per day. There was, to be sure, the bounty money to be added to the two months' pay. The camp must have overflowed with tobacco and whiskey.

Food seems to have been fairly plentiful in the camp late in 1861 but of very poor quality and even poorer preparation. However, men were coming and going constantly between the camp and home. Someone was arriving in camp or returned home every week. These men brought letters and "boxes" of food and clothing to relatives and friends. For a while after an arrival any lucky man and his friends ate well. Fresh meat, especially pork and possum, butter, eggs, bread, wheat coffee (since the real thing was almost impossible to secure) and other delights from home would have been in those boxes.

Around Christmas 1861, Louis McLeod got leave to return home for a few days to do some recruiting. He returned to camp in January with three men and wrote to Eliza that one of his cousins had come down at the same time with "speculation chickens." Andrew Brown[40] was a well-to-do farmer who lived in Chatham County just over the line from McLeod in Moore County (both areas now part of Lee County). Brown brought with him an enormous coop of chickens so large that McLeod was told it took 13 Negroes to lift it on and off the boat that steamed down the Cape Fear River. The number of laborers sounds exaggerated but no doubt Brown had brought many chickens with him. The captain of the river boat that Brown and McLeod boarded in Fayetteville at first praised Brown for his devotion to the troops. When the captain learned the chickens were "a speculation" and not a gift, Brown was charged a high tariff. Eliza wrote that people in Moore County were outraged. Rumors were flying that Brown had taken whiskey to sell by the dram and backbone and spare ribs to sell at a high price. The only certain thing is that he took chickens for his son and friends, members of Company H, to sell for profit. McLeod reported that he didn't think it worked out so well for cousin Andrew, because so many others had had similar ideas that the camp had a glut of chickens.

For six months, the men engaged in a pretend war. Still poorly trained, they had not encountered any Union troops. They were living in small houses, often fairly well-furnished with many of the comforts of home. In the spring of 1862, things quickly changed.

4

Conscription and Discipline

By the spring of 1862 after nine months of training, the 30th North Carolina was equipped, able to do battalion drill and form a line of battle. It had yet to be blooded and was in no real sense a fighting unit. The task of making these farmers who could march into real soldiers fell to General Samuel B. French.

General French was a native of New Jersey and veteran of the Mexican War who had bought a large cotton plantation in Mississippi around 1850. He accepted command of the Mississippi State Army in 1861 and quickly was promoted to brigadier general in the Confederate Army.[1] He was ordered to North Carolina in early 1862 to take charge of the defense of New Bern and of Kinston. By the time he arrived on 17 March, New Bern had fallen to General Burnside. On 20 March under new orders, he took command of forces at Wilmington. Most of General French's time would be occupied with increasing fortifications and defenses at Wilmington and especially at Fort Fisher. He did not, however, neglect the 30th North Carolina and was determined that the men would become real, rather than pretend, soldiers. The process began with a lot of walking and moving.

General French ordered the regiment at the end of March to the outskirts of Wilmington where one company was put on picket duty and the other nine bivouacked near the breastworks thrown up to defend the small city.[2] General French placed the men in tents. In his opinion soldiers had no need of houses. He also ordered all boxes and baggage sent home. He told Colonel Parker that he intended on moving the regiment vigorously and with great frequency until they lost all superfluous baggage.[3] He wanted them ready to march quickly and at length on a moment's notice. Colonel Parker at once set the example by sending home all of his excess baggage. On 30 or 31 March, General French ordered the regiment to march five miles to Camp Holmes near the Masonboro Sound.

In mid–April it seemed the 30th would at last face the enemy. On 18 April, Companies A, D and H were sent as lead units of the regiment to Onslow County to defend against Union raiding parties. Colonel Parker made a stirring exhortation, describing the Union Army as probable rapists, the cruelest of villains. Evidently many of the men were brought to tears with the emotion of the occasion. Here is how one soldier reported the address:

> Fellow suldiers you are a going to meet the enemy to drive them back. your hard ships is grate but gest look at your homes your wives your daughters your sisters How they would serve them. When they take a man down here they will tye him & whip him and tar him & feather him. Hoo can stand that When you strike strike deep & drive them devils back. Now is the time to do it. the nireer the time comes to go the worse I want to go The van Company is gone & we will soon follow you.[4]

On 20 April the other companies, save one on picket duty in Wilmington, followed to Onslow County. By 21 April, Companies A, D and H were at Jacksonville and on 24 April at Hatchels Mills where they were joined by the other six companies. The regiment, still minus one company, moved to Camp Sanders on the White Oak River and set up camp. They named the camp after an old woman who had been "mistreated" by Union raiders.[5] A.F. Harrington heard the woman's story and wrote about how sorry they all felt for her.

> She told us how the yankeys served her. thare was 100 of them went to her house of cavalry. she was in the kitchen when they come & the Captain raised up in his stirups & shucked his sword over her & told her to go in to the house like she would tell her nigers then made her give up her keys & then took her juelry[,] one gole sketch rings[,] bed close[,] sugar & coffee & money[,] 7 mules & 7 horses[,] wagons & cart cariages 6 negro men[.] ... I never was so sorry for a woman in my life she was acrying when she was a talking.[6]

During the last week of April and into May 1862, the regiment moved back and forth several times but never saw any Yankees. General French was implementing his plan to harden them. It would seem, however, that at least one company of the regiment still did not understand that they were no longer free to do as they pleased. Company A had originally formed on 20 April 1861 as a cavalry unit expecting to be assigned to the 20th North Carolina Regiment. Instead it was assigned to the 30th as an infantry company. On 20 April 1862, Company A was one of the first to extend its term of service but, the men insisted, with conditions. They agreed to stay for two years or for the war, but only as a cavalry unit. After the re-enlistment, the men reelected all company officers except one,[7] were paid the extra $50 bounty and furloughed home. However, with the danger posed by Union troops after the fall of New Bern, the men were ordered back to camp at once and were then placed on constant duty. In the second week of May, Captain Holmes[8] wrote to the Secretary of War complaining of the canceled furloughs. He insisted that the company had re-enlisted only as a cavalry company and demanded to be transferred as such.[9] Colonel Parker signed off on the letter but requested that Company A not leave until it could be replaced. The letter then went to General French's desk. His response was decidedly unsympathetic.

General French assumed, perhaps correctly, that the major reason Company A wanted to be a cavalry unit was they believed they would be assigned to duty close to home. He dismissed the petition out of hand. First, there was already a sufficiency of mounted troops in eastern North Carolina. Second, the general expressed his firm belief that it was always a mistake for troops to be within 500 miles of home. The more distance from home they were assigned, the better. Furthermore, Company A was completely undeserving of any consideration for the men had disobeyed direct orders. General French wrote that he had been informed that when he ordered the regiment to Onslow County, Company A "while on the march [sic] stacked their arms and refused to proceed any further for a time, because on that day their term of service as infantry [sic] expired."[10] Nothing more was heard of the request to become cavalry.

No matter how well-trained, equipped, and obedient the men might have been after absorbing General French's lessons, there was a very pressing problem that could dissolve the regiment before it ever fought—each man had volunteered for 12 months and that time was running out.

Expectations of Short War

"We will plow over this war before August and go home."
—Andrew Brown

It is a near certainty that few men volunteer for a war they expect to lose. It has been noted by historians many times that most young volunteers, who have never been in war, expect to have a short victorious march to the end accompanied by the cheers of family and the tears and embraces of girls. The Civil War is a perfect example.

The men of the 30th North Carolina volunteered for 12 months of service. The expectation was there would be some training; the Yankees would invade eastern North Carolina. They would be driven out again and the war would be finished. At the beginning of October 1861, some thought the fighting "was all done," so Louis McLeod wrote his wife on 2 October. By December, Union ships could be seen off the coast and it seemed that the Union indeed would land troops. But there were so many men at or near Camp Wyatt, two entire regiments, that Louis McLeod was certain they could drive any Yankee attack away easily. The actual number of men present would have been about 1,500 which seemed to the North Carolina volunteers an enormous number. In truth, 1,500 was not, as events would prove, enough even to slow the Yankees, much less drive them away. In addition, of course, the number of men away or unable to perform duty due to sickness, arrest or furlough was so large so that Colonel Parker felt the regiment "would make but a poor resistance to the enemy should they attempt to land."[11] None of this dampened the confidence of the men. A.F. Harrington wrote his nephew J.K.P. Harrington on 23 April 1862 that Andrew Brown[12] says "we will plow over this war before August and go home."

With things looking so easy, young men who wanted to participate felt that they must volunteer quickly or miss the war altogether. This was the case with the Goodin family of Wake County.[13] Willis Goodin, aged 20, and his brother John C. Goodin, aged 18, signed up at once as members of Company D, 30th North Carolina on 2 September 1861. On 13 February 1862, their half-brother Wesley Brassfield, aged 35, joined them. A younger brother, Joseph J. Goodin, came to

Camp Wyatt and asked to join. He was only 16 or 17. Captain Grissom told him that he was taking no more volunteers and sent him home, probably because of his age. The war, of course, waited for Joseph Goodin. He was drafted and became a member of Company D, 30th North Carolina on 20 March 1864 when he was 19. His brothers were not there to greet him. Willis had died in August 1862 of typhoid, John had been killed at Gettysburg and Wesley Brassfield had been captured and imprisoned at Point Lookout, Maryland, where he died of chronic diarrhea on 12 February 1864.

In the fall of 1861, the news from Virginia seemed to confirm the view of a short, victorious war. After all, had not the Yankees been destroyed at Manassas and each encounter afterwards, especially those led by the great Stonewall Jackson, demonstrated the invincibility of the Confederacy? W.E. Ardrey of Company K noted all these victories in his diary. Of course, as we have already seen, the news from nearby was not so good. By mid–February, General Burnside had taken Hatteras, Roanoke Island, landed on the mainland and on 14 March New Bern fell to Union forces. On 26 April, Fort Macon surrendered with seven Confederates dead and 400 taken prisoner, or so W.E. Ardrey was told. North Carolina seemed almost helpless to resist the Union invasion. Lieutenant William Sillers, Company A, wrote to his sister, "It will take many hard successive victories of no mean account to pay for the defeats we have lately suffered."[14] The view was that the loss of Roanoke Island was inexcusable, and some thought those troops who were there were not up to what they should have been.

At home the fear of loss quickly became pronounced. Eliza McLeod wrote to Louis on 25 February that people in Moore County feared defeat. The news of Roanoke was terrifying. She wrote that opinion was that if England and France didn't soon join the South, "We will have to give up." She was in terror that they would be "a conquered people."[15]

The war now looked as if it would go beyond one year. The volunteers of 1861, however, were already near the end of their enlistment, and there was no groundswell of additional volunteers. The Confederacy was in a predicament of its own creation. Units like the 30th North Carolina were on the verge of disbanding without ever having met the enemy.

In for the War

> *"I don't think any in the company will go in for the war."*
> —Louis McLeod

From the beginning of the war some Confederate leaders had been urging total mobilization of manpower as the only way to victory. D.H. Hill wrote so many letters and newspaper pieces in 1861 on the subject that his wife asked him to stop.[16] People in North Carolina were very critical of him for calling for that, she said. No one wanted to have such a policy and no one liked hearing or reading such words. Hill, of course, continued to urge mobilization knowing the alternative was sure defeat.

By the early spring of 1862, Confederate authorities were moving in the direction of Hill's views but not, it would seem, very far or fast. Small, reluctant steps were taken to build up the armed forces. First a campaign was launched to convince the units already under arms to extend enlistment from 12 months to the duration of the war. The push focused on seeking a unanimous re-enlistment within each company. This met with limited success. In the 30th, Companies A and E quickly signed on though as we have seen, Company A intended to leave the 30th and become cavalry. The captains of the two companies, James C. Holmes and John C. McMillan,[17] were highly respected and were able to convince their troops. To reward those companies, the men were given a long furlough home. Within other companies there was considerable resistance to the idea. Companies D and H resisted strongly.[18]

When patriotic entreaties and pleas of group unity failed to convince, North Carolina added a $100 bounty in addition to a 30-day furlough. If the entire regiment signed up, each company would hold an election to re-organize itself. The newly elected company officers would reelect regimental officers. Still, many men resisted. McLeod wrote both his wife and John Harrington that not many in Company H were willing to sign on. They felt they had done their duty and others at home had made no sacrifice. By early April McLeod wrote that men in Company H would wait until their enlistment was up in September. If the war was still going on, they would re-enlist for the duration.

Resistance to extending for the war was intense in Company K where officers apparently disliked each other and openly expressed their antagonism. Some talked of leaving the 30th to form a new company in some other regiment. One of the leaders of the near insurrection in Company K was John Witherspoon. He encouraged his brother and friends to solicit volunteers for a new company with himself as an officer, preferably captain. He felt sure he could bring some men of Company K with him.[19] Nothing came of the agitation, perhaps because the old captain of Company K, Benjamin Morrow,[20] was turned out and Witherspoon elected the new captain. One can only imagine what would have been General French's response had the threats to leave reached him.

By May, resistance to re-enlistment weakened under constant pressure and the thought of 30 days at home and, above all, the $100 (actually $90 since $10 was kept to cover some expenses). One hundred dollars was, as McLeod put it, "more than a heap of them can make in a year or two." Eliza McLeod wrote tearful letters begging Louis not to re-enlist. His family had suffered enough. He had done more than his part, she said. Let some of the others take a turn.

State officials came to speak, and Colonel Parker entreated. In the end, much to Eliza McLeod's sorrow, her husband and the entire company signed on. The bounty was quickly paid and sent home or spent in Wilmington. However, the promised 30-day furlough, which had swayed many men, was never given. The colonel, of course, could not send new companies on furlough until the companies already furloughed had returned to camp. By the time that happened, the 30th North Carolina was in Virginia and furloughs became non-existent.

Enlisted men may have had great reservations about extending beyond 12 months, but the Confederate Congress did not. By February 1862, it was becoming clear that even retaining those original units for the duration would not suffice. Lincoln was raising division upon division of volunteers, and the South had to do the same or lose the war. So on 16 April 1862, the Confederate Congress passed its first conscription law. The law also extended terms of service for those already in the army from one to three years. Therefore, it mattered not at all whether the men of the 30th wished to extend. They were extended. Companies and regiments could be reorganized. All white males 18–35, except for those with exemptions, were now subject to draft. The law made it somewhat more difficult to hire a substitute in that the man hired had to be older than 35 or have some other exemption to the draft. Each state was given a quota and told to organize its draft.[21] Many in North Carolina were very opposed to conscription; this law and subsequent conscription acts were fought in North Carolina courts.[22]

North Carolina scheduled a draft for late April 1862. It was organized by county, and new units would first be formed by seeking volunteers and then a draft would complete the needed manpower. The exemptions were numerous, and to the modern mind blatantly based on status and wealth. Among others, millers, tanners, teachers of 20 or more pupils, government clerks, mail carriers, ferrymen, ministers, iron workers, printers, college professors and superintendents in wool or cotton factories were all excluded from service. The most notorious exemption was for any man who owned, or was the only white man working, 20 or more slaves. The justification was the necessity for growing food and cotton.[23] But there were lesser known exemptions. A.F. Harrington's oldest brother James[24] had enough political influence to have his dwelling designated a post office and his oldest son named postmaster. The position carried exemption from the draft. A.F.'s brother John sent his second son to Fayetteville to work as a printer for a newspaper as soon as he was of age. John's older son, James K.P. Harrington, had volunteered at the age of 18 and served 1862–1865 in the cavalry.

If you could not find an exemption for yourself or your son, it was acceptable to pay someone to replace the drafted person. The most common price paid a substitute early in 1862 was $100, at least a year's wages in pre-war money. There were rumors, according to one letter received by McLeod, that some were offering as much as $500.[25] When conscription day came in Moore County, an appeal was made for volunteers; money was offered to increase the bounty. James Kelly[26] announced he was raising a company and invited men to join him. Only a few responded, and the draft was held at once. Many men who could not secure an exemption or who could not afford to pay a substitute were conscripted. Some of the unlucky joined James Kelly's company which became Company F of the 50th North Carolina. Others drafted were assigned to various units within a few weeks.

North Carolinians talked a lot about conscription in the weeks leading up to the actual event. Opinion was sharply divided. Some approved in patriotic fervor. Other men were public in denouncing the process and in declaring they intended to fight any attempt to force them into the army. Eliza McLeod told Louis about men who were rumored to have injured themselves to avoid going.[27] A friend, with considerable disgust, sent Louis McLeod a list of local men who refused to volunteer or participate in the draft.[28]

In the reorganization of companies in the 30th on 1 May 1862, most of the original officers were reelected.[29] But in some companies, and Company H was one, old officers were voted out and new ones chosen. William Swann had lost the confidence of his men partly because he had gone home in April and stayed weeks longer than he should have. In fact, he was not even back in camp when the election was held.[30] The new captain was Jesse Wicker.[31] In addition, the original lieutenants, Archibald McIntosh[32] (1st Lieutenant), Daniel W. McIntosh[33] (2nd Lieutenant) and Francis Moore (2nd Lieutenant), were not reelected. The new 1st lieutenant was Henry J. McNeill[34]; the 2nd lieutenants were Archibald A. Jackson[35] and Louis McLeod.

The regiment also reorganized on 1 May 1862, and there were changes. Colonel Francis Parker was confirmed but Lt. Colonel Walter Draughan was defeated and replaced by Major James T. Kell (in September 1861 Captain of Company K). William W. Sillers (1st Lieutenant of Company A) was elected major. Personnel changes were made in the regimental staff which would be maintained for most of the war.

In the spring of 1862, the regiment was as well-supplied and trained as it could be. It had, at last, been issued uniforms. Louis McLeod told his wife with great pride that they had splendid uniforms of the best cloth with brown pants and everything lined with Osnaburg cloth. Everyone in Company H, save McLeod and one other man, had gotten caps.[36]

Before the 30th could actually go to war, however, there were some final necessities to be added. Much of this work fell on Regimental Quartermaster Buckner D. Williams.[37] In May of 1862 when the regiment was at Camp Lamb, he went to Wilmington and bought teams to pull the regiment's wagons.[38] He returned with 24 mules. From this point on he had to requisition each month food for the mules, six public horses and a large number of private horses belonging to officers and surgeons of the regiment. To take only one example, on 1 October 1862, Williams requisitioned food for the 30 public animals: 7,344 lbs. corn, 1,500 lbs. oats, 9,421 lbs. hay and 2,700 lbs. wheat. For the next two years, the overall amount requisitioned was fairly constant but varied depending on what was available of corn, oats, hay, wheat or fodder. In December 1862, he noted that he could not obtain full rations for the animals, receiving only 11,160 lbs. corn, 550 lbs. oats and 7,250 lbs. fodder. The exact number of animals also varied some depending on deaths and available supplies. For June 1863, for example, Williams requisitioned for one horse and 28 mules. What is certain is that without the animals and wagons the regiment could not function. At the end of May when the regiment was on the move in eastern North Carolina, according to Louis McLeod, it took 30 to 35 wagons to move the regiment if they were moving too far for the wagons to make two trips.[39]

When the regiment left North Carolina for Virginia, the outfitting was complete. On 14 June 1862, Buckner Williams signed a receipt for $30,100, the amount of money he estimated was needed for pay, forage and clothing for the regiment. At last the regiment was fully equipped and ready for war. The war they would find, however, was not the war they expected. In fact they had already met an enemy that would prove to be far more dangerous than Union soldiers. It was an enemy that even the most knowledgeable men did not comprehend—disease.

5

The Big Man's War
Fought by the Little Man

*"I want to see the Big men come out a while & take my
fare I think this ware will stop then That is all the way I
see to bring it to an end."*
—A.F. Harrington, January 1864

Who were the men of the 30th North Carolina? If we are going
to see them as real men and not just the unsmiling, mostly bearded
men of 1862 photographs, we must go deeper into the sources. *NC
Troops* and military documents from the National Archives will tell
us much—how old were they, were they literate enough to write their
names, how tall were they, what was their typical coloring, where did
they live when they enlisted? We can know far more. Were they married, did they have children? What were their economic and social
backgrounds?

Perhaps the most important question is whether the Civil War
was, as many men and older historians charged, a big man's war and
a little man's fight.[1] Today the view has changed. One might even say
it has become fashionable to argue as does Joseph T. Glatthaar, "This
was not ... a rich man's war and a poor man's fight.... It was a rich,
moderate, and poor man's fight."[2] Aaron Sheehan-Dean maintains that
the well-to-do in Virginia were over-represented in the Confederate
Army.[3] Colin Woodward agrees that the rich, driven by their desire to
maintain slavery, were heavily represented in the Confederate Army.
He insists the ratio of slave owners was higher than in the South as a
whole.[4] These three excellent historians all believe that the rich volunteered and served in high numbers. Certainly there were rich men who
fought. They did so in the 30th. However, if a historian argues the rich

fought in numbers proportional to the poor, she must prove the point decisively. In every American war from the Revolution to Vietnam, the rich easily found ways to avoid fighting and dying as they cheered on the poor. These three historians have written masterful books based on extensive research and many years of study and writing on the Civil War. Even so, on this point at least, I find myself strongly disagreeing. The recent work of Keri Leigh Merritt on poor whites' forced participation in the war, on the other hand, fits very well with what the data on the 30th North Carolina show.[5] Let us delay a response to the big man/little man question until we examine the economic data on the 30th North Carolina.

The best source for social and economic data on the men of the 30th is the eighth population census of the United Stated taken in 1860. It listed each member of free households, gave the value of real estate and personal property owned, occupation, place of birth and some other miscellaneous information such as literacy or idiocy. Enslaved people were listed on a separate census schedule with only the owner and age and sex of slaves. The 1860 census should give us exactly the information needed for examining the social status of individuals. The most serious problem is that many people are simply missing, either because the census taker failed to enumerate them or because the forms have disappeared. For example, William Swann was elected captain of Company H when it formed in Moore County in 1861. The Swann family was a prominent one with large land holdings and slaves (34 according the slave schedule which is extant) and a store at what had been the temporary end of the Western Railroad in 1860. The entire family is missing from both the 1860 and 1850 census though not from the slave schedule.[6] There are other problems of inconsistent terms and uncertainty about how census takers estimated wealth. Merritt believes that 10 to 15 percent of poor whites were not listed.[7] Nevertheless, the census remains the best source. Over half of the men of the 30th North Carolina (880) have been identified in the 1860 census schedule.

Believing that any information is better than no information, we searched the 1850 census for all men not found in the 1860 census. This provides data on another 206 men. Most were children in 1850 but at least we know the social and economic level of their families.[8] In addition, we have found occupations for 58 men missing from both sets of census records in other documents, for example in the personal records kept in the National Archives. We have, therefore, identified by occupation 1,144 men, well over two-thirds of the regiment.

The dilemma when considering wealth and social status is how best to arrange the data. There are no generally accepted criteria; in a real sense each study is *sui generis*. After much consideration I decided to sort the men into six categories: Laborer; Small Farmer; Craftsman or Mechanic; Middling Farmer; Professional; or Wealthy Farmer. Naturally because many of the volunteers in 1861 were aged 17–25, the 1860 census returns show that a high percentage were unmarried and still lived at the family home. I have assigned such men the wealth of the head of the family as more representative of actual status. In some cases, sons of fairly prosperous farmers were called farm hands or farm laborers in the census. These men are more accurately listed with the status of the father, and we have so arranged them.

Before presenting the data, there is a need to delve into the how the six categories are defined and why. The question of what indicated levels of wealth in the past is extremely contentious. Disagreement is widespread. Joseph Glatthaar, in his groundbreaking study of a sample of 600 men in the Army of Northern Virginia, chose to see men as falling into three broad categories: poor men with less wealth than $800; middling from $800 to $3,999; and wealthy men with wealth in excess of $4,000.[9] After studying the men of the 30th, I find Glatthaar's categories unhelpful. Keri Merritt is on this question much more in tune with social reality. She counts as poor all those who own less than $100 of property.[10] I have used a different set of categories which I believe more accurately describes North Carolina reality. Glatthaar, however, does not limit his analyses to three simple categories. His description and charts present the data in far more complex ways. I have, therefore, analyzed the men of the 30th in a second way in order to compare them with Glatthaar's data.

Laborers

Nearly 25 percent of the men in our sample owned no land and little or no personal property. They were totally dependent on paid physical labor for their survival. According to statistics published by the Census Bureau and drawn from the 1860 census, North Carolinians were paid among the lowest wages in the country. Average wages for a day laborer with board were $.54 per day; average wages for a day laborer without board were $.77. If a laborer was fortunate enough to have a job paying monthly wages with board, he was paid, on average, $10.37.[11] The average weekly cost for laborers who paid for board was $1.84; nearly two and one-half days' wages. It is interesting to note that weekly wages with board for a female domestic were $1.08, exactly one-third of a male laborer's wages assuming a six-day work week. Of course we do not know how many days on average a laborer was able to work in a year. It must have varied considerably by season and weather. What is clear is that a $50 or $100 bounty to a recruit, or a North Carolina substitute, represented a considerable amount of money. A private in the Confederate Army was paid $11 per month in addition to food and shelter. That was better than the average wage before the war.

Our sample identifies 255 men (23.6 percent) as Laborers. They included: 15 day laborers, 18 farm hands, 101 farm laborers, 92 laborers, seven railroad laborers, 13 turpentine laborers, seven turpentiners, one land renter and one man in jail (in 1860) for resisting arrest. At the same time, there are 35 men found in the 1860 census called farmers who own no property of any kind, and 44 men who are sons of property-less farmers in the 1850 census. There is a very high likelihood that these men were tenant farmers or sharecroppers of some sort. Almost certainly they had more to do with labor than independent farming, and I have classified them as Labor in this study. This gives a total of 334 men, or 29.3 percent of the regiment, who earned their living entirely by labor at very low wages.

Professor Glatthaar reports 35.8 percent of infantrymen in the Army of Northern Virginia had property worth less than $400.[12]

I have divided farmers who owned property into Small Farmers, Middling Farmers and Wealthy Farmers (planters). The division and labels are admittedly rather arbitrary, but I believe it reflects the social reality of the 30th. It is certain that the men themselves considered that some were "big men" with considerable resources as opposed to "little men." The Confederate Congress often used the number of 20 slaves as being an important number. I chose levels of wealth that seem to make sense given information on property and slaves and the attitudes of the men themselves.

Small Farmers

The poorest among these men owned no real estate and personal property of only $5. The upper limit is set at total property of $5,000 in 1860 (real estate of at least $500 in 1850 census) and no more than eight slaves. Three to eight slaves on a farm often represented one slave family and included young children and would represent personal property of roughly $5,000. These families were self-sufficient, most without slave labor. Certainly the upper limit of eight slaves would merge into the next level of wealth, but such is always true of descriptive boundaries. The 1860 census identifies 294 men who fit the criteria while the 1850 census adds 42 more. In addition, other sources indicate an additional 61 men with comparable status. The best estimate is that 397 men, or 35 percent, fall into this category.

Middling Farmers

These men owned total property between $5,000 and $25,000 in 1860 or owned between nine and 25 slaves (real estate from $500–$5,000 in 1850 or six to 15 slaves). These men most often owned slaves and were literate, and their personal property indicated some luxuries. One hundred and fifty-six men (102 in 1860 and 36 in 1850), 14.4 percent, would be called Middling Farmers.

Wealthy Farmers

These men, who owned more than $25,000 in total property in 1860 or more than 25 slaves (real estate of more than $5,000 or more than 15 slaves in 1850), were the true elite. They owned large numbers of slaves, and many were college educated. Fifty-six men (50 in 1860, five in 1850 and one from the archives) or 4.9 percent were in this elite group.

To complete our list of those engaged in agriculture we must add two farm managers and 16 overseers, men who should be considered at the level of Small Farmers save one who owned 11 slaves. The totals for those primarily engaged in agriculture or hand labor of some sort: Laborers 334 (29.5 percent); Small Farmers and over-seers 413 (36.4 percent); Middling Farmers 156 (14.4 percent); and Wealthy Farmers or planters 56 (5 percent). Thus, 85.3 percent of men in the 30th North Carolina were primarily engaged in agriculture at some level.

Only 14.7 percent of the men in the 30th North Carolina made their primary living from non-agricultural work and even some of those, physicians and lawyers for example, also owned land and slaves and profited from agriculture. These men easily fit into the same patterns as their agricultural friends. We sort them as follows: Craftsmen or Mechanics, including apprentices, comparable to Small Farmers; Mid-level, made up of clerks, government officials, students and teachers (mostly children of professionals or wealthy farmers) and small merchants comparable to Middling Farmers; and Professionals and large merchants who are comparable to Wealthy Farmers in status. One clear indication that mechanics and craftsmen were of a higher status than laborers is that the average day wage without board for a carpenter in North Carolina in 1860 was $1.56, more than double that of a laborer. Ninety-four men can be identified as Craftsmen of some sort.[13] At the Mid-level, seven were clerks; six were government officials, mostly constables and deputy sheriffs and 40 were students or teachers. Twenty-four were Professionals or large merchants including one liquor dealer, three lawyers, one clergyman and three physicians. In sum, 29.3 percent of the 30th were Laborers; 44.3 percent were Small Farmers or Craftsmen; 18.3 percent were Middling Farmers or their non-agricultural equivalents; and 7.4 percent were Wealthy Farmers or Professionals.

Some historians, including Professor Glatthaar, would call all my Middling Farmers and even a good number of my Small Farmers wealthy. The men themselves would more likely have agreed with my descriptions. Sergeant A.F. Harrington's letters in 1864 and 1865 are bitter that the "big men" are not fighting or even supporting the war. In 1860, he owned $2,000 of real estate and $5,000 of personal property, including three slaves. He would have been astonished at being considered one of the big men.

Before leaving the question of overall wealth, let us compare the men of the 30th North Carolina with infantrymen of the Army of Northern Virginia.[14] The following chart in Figure 2 compares

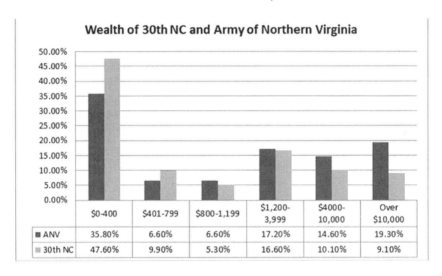

Figure 2. Overall Family Wealth of Soldiers

combined real estate and personal property of men found in the 1860 census using Professor Glatthaar's economic boundaries.

If Professor Glatthaar's sample is accurate, the men of the 30th North Carolina seem to have been less well-to-do than the infantry of the army as a whole. The differences are most apparent in numbers for the poorest and the richest.

It is not surprising when we look at social status by military rank (Figure 3) that we find sharp differences of wealth. Eight hundred and forty men in our sample held no rank higher than private. Three hundred and five (36.3 percent) were Laborers; 368 (43.8 percent) were Small Farmers or Craftsmen; 130 (15.5 percent) were Middling Farmers; and 37 (4.4 percent) were Wealthy Farmers or Professionals.

Among men who were elected or promoted to non-commissioned officer rank, 28 (11.8 percent) were Laborers; 65 (42.5 percent) were Craftsmen or Small Farmers; 47 (30.7 percent) were Middling Farmers; and 13 (8.5 percent) were Wealthy Farmers or Professionals.

The correlation between wealth and rank is even more pronounced in commissioned officers. Forty-nine men were elected or promoted to 3rd, 2nd or 1st lieutenant. Fourteen (28.6 percent) of the lieutenants were Wealthy Farmers or Professionals; 18 (36.7 percent) were Middling Farmers; 11 (22.4 percent) were Craftsmen or Small Farmers; and only six (12.2 percent) were Laborers. Twenty captains

	Privates	NCO	Lieutenants	Captains	Field and Staff
Laborers	36.3%	11.8%	12.2%		
Small Farmers Or Craftsmen	43.8%	42.5%	22.4%	10%	
Middling Farmer	15.5%	40.7%	36.7%	50%	
Wealthy Farmers or Professionals	4.4%	8.5%	28.6%	40%	100%

Figure 3. Social Class by Military Rank

were included in the sample. There were no Laborers among them. Two were Small Farmers, 10 were Middling Farmers and eight were Wealthy Farmers. All field and staff officers came from the Wealthy Farmer or Professional class.

In military matters as in politics and local society, men of means were assumed to be the natural leaders. Men of no means were assumed to be fit mostly to follow.

Slavery

In a very real sense the South fought in 1861 to preserve slavery. Attitudes about slavery and people of color among the 30th will be discussed in the next chapter, but the question of how many men of the 30th North Carolina owned slaves is very pertinent to social status and wealth. The 1860 census reported that in slave states, 4.9 percent of adults and 24.9 percent of free households owned slaves. In North Carolina as a whole, 27 percent of free families owned slaves. Overall in North Carolina 67 percent of slave holders owned less than 10 slaves. The men of the 30th came from all parts of North Carolina—from western counties where slavery was almost non-existent and eastern counties like Duplin and Nash with large enslaved populations. Moore County, home of the majority of Company H, was geographically in the center of the state and in the middle of slave owning as well. In Moore County, 468 free households, roughly one-quarter of the total, owned slaves; however, 294 of them (63 percent of slave owners) owned one to four slaves.[15]

45

How does the 30th compare with North Carolina and infantry-men in the Army of Northern Virginia? The most accurate data for the 30th are on the 880 men found in the 1860 and 1850 census returns. The overwhelming majority, 722 men (82 percent), appear to belong to families which owned no slaves.[16] Sixty-four men (7.3 percent) owned one to eight slaves; 57 (6.5 percent) owned nine to 25 slaves; 34 (3.9 percent) owned 26 or more slaves. The men of the 30th were certainly less involved in slavery than the average North Carolinian.

In order to compare the 30th North Carolina with the infantry-men of the Army of Northern Virginia, I took the 694 men found in the 1860 census, using again family data rather than individual. The lack of slave owning in the regiment compared to Professor Glatthaar's data on the Army of Northern Virginia is in line with differences in overall wealth (Figure 4). In the 30th, 88 percent owned no slaves; 1.4 percent owned one or two slaves; 4.9 percent owned three to ten slaves; 2.9 percent owned 11 to 19 slaves; only 2.6 percent owned 20 or more slaves.

We will discuss motivations in a later chapter. However, it is worth noting here that more than 80 percent of the regiment were in fact fighting to maintain an institution, slavery, in which they had no direct economic interest.

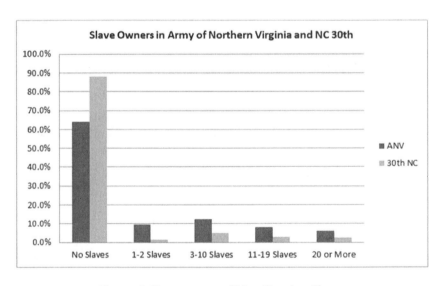

Figure 4. Percentages of Men Owning Slaves

The men of the 30th do not resemble the data presented by Professor Glatthaar for infantrymen of the Army of Northern Virginia. This, in itself, is no reason to doubt his data. The 30th may have been an aberration or simply different from the average. Certainly each regiment was unique. It does, however, give pause.

Substitutes

There is a final way in which the idea of little men fighting the big man's war is apparent—substitutes.[17] During the first half of the war both Union and Confederate armies provided for a man to be able to pay another to substitute for him. The substitute could be hired at any point, even after a man was in the army.[18] After the passage of the first Confederate Conscription Act, a substitute had to be a man not subject to conscription. We have identified 20 substitutes in the 30th though it is possible that there were more.[19] These men are interesting for several reasons. First, six of them replaced men who volunteered and wished to leave the unit for some reason before the 30th saw combat and before the Conscription Act set age requirements. The last month that substitutes could be hired was June 1863, and two agreed to serve in that month. After the summer of 1863 the Confederate Congress, as we have seen, eliminated substitutes.[20]

What is most striking about substitutes is their age. Of course after the first Conscription Law was passed only those over 35 were eligible. Six of the substitutes in the 30th took money before that law and were under 25 years old. Eight were men in their 50s. The average age of a recruit in 1861 was 24; the average age of a substitute was 40. The obvious question is why did these older men, the majority of whom were too old to be drafted, sign on as substitutes? The simple answer is, of course, for the money. However, the answer is more nuanced than that. Eleven of the 20 men appear in the 1860 census schedules. Six of the 11 are laborers with large families. It is impossible to know what these men were paid to substitute but in the McLeod letters, $500 and even $1,000 are mentioned.[21] This represented to a typical laborer as much as 10- to 20-years' pay. Why would a 58-year-old mechanic/laborer with five children substitute for a wealthy man? It would seem clear that it was a way of providing for his family. He could not hope to live much longer in any event and as an old soldier, death was a near certainty. It would not be a distortion to see being a substitute as insurance for the family. In some cases this was re-enforced by an agreement that the man who paid the substitute would provide for the substitute's children in case of death.[22] The fate of the older substitutes is what one would expect. As a group, however, substitutes suffered casualties in similar percentages as the regiment as a whole: eight died; two deserted; two finished the war as POWs; one was hospitalized; one was discharged as being over-aged; two surrendered at Appomattox.

Wealth

Let us now return to the question of big man/little man in the light of the data on the 30th and that presented by Joseph T. Glatthaar, Aaron Sheehan-Dean, and Colin Woodward.

Professor Glatthaar's book is the culmination of decades of research into the Army of Northern Virginia. I have already shown in this chapter how the 30th North Carolina was much different from the numbers presented in *Soldiering in the Army of Northern Virginia*. It is, of course, possible that the 30th was very different than many other regiments. It is possible that it was atypical of the Army of Northern Virginia. I doubt it. I fear it is far more likely that Professor's Glatthaar's sample is not as valid as he believed. His methodology is exact, but the size of the sample—only 600 men, of which 300 are infantry—gives pause. It is not just in questions of wealth, but in other areas such as death rates from various causes, that the sample seems to fail. I will return to that question in a later chapter.

The question of wealth is not the main focus of *Why Confederates Fought*. The book is more concerned with motivation and support for the Confederacy. However, Professor Sheehan-Dean presents a strong argument that, in Virginia at least, the rich volunteered in very great numbers, in some counties more than poorer men. There are problems with this view. First, like *Soldiering*, it is based on sampling, but unlike *Soldiering* is very short on statistics and charts. Second, the book, aside from slave owning, never really defines what is meant by various descriptive terms for wealth. It is especially frustrating to read the term "middle class" tossed about frequently but never defined. What that might mean for an agricultural, slave-owning society in 1860 is difficult to imagine. Third, the book really deals with Virginia, not the South as a whole. It is, therefore, quite possible that the conclusions are totally valid for Virginia, but not necessarily for the rest of the Confederacy. The author does, however, state strongly his belief that the conclusions are valid beyond Virginia's borders. Let me offer two sets of data from the 30th which tend to cast doubt on the rich fully participating in the war.

Professor Sheehan-Dean writes, accurately I believe, that many men of means and wealth volunteered. They certainly did in North Carolina as well, especially in 1861. However, the question I would pose is: how long did they remain? Men who were not reelected company or regimental officers in May 1862, before the 30th saw combat, were permitted to resign and leave the army, unlike enlisted men. In the 30th North Carolina, 19 men resigned and left the unit in May 1862. Another 13 men left during the same period by paying a substitute. Fourteen more transferred to other units away from the front. This accounts for only 3 percent of the total enrollment in the regiment. However, they represent 5 percent of the original volunteers. This speaks very much to the question of big versus little men. Of these men, 39 appear in the 1860 census. Figure 5 shows the wealth of these men relative to the 30th as a whole and to Professor Glatthaar's data for wealth in the infantry of the Army of Northern Virginia. There is no doubt those who left were overwhelmingly "big men." The average wealth of the men who resigned in May 1862 was $28,411; at the top was a man worth $103,000. The fact that they volunteered is negated by their early exit. If a great many companies in Virginia exhibit similar data, then the question of big men fighting has not been settled at all.

There is a second and broader way to shed some light on whether big men left the army in greater numbers than little men. Figure 6, using Glatthaar's classification of wealth, shows percentages among early volunteers in 1861 and percentages still with the 30th North Carolina on 1 January 1865.

The data make several things clear. The well-to-do did volunteer in considerable numbers in 1861. They did not do so in 1862 and 1863, perhaps taking advantage of the many exemptions to the draft. Their

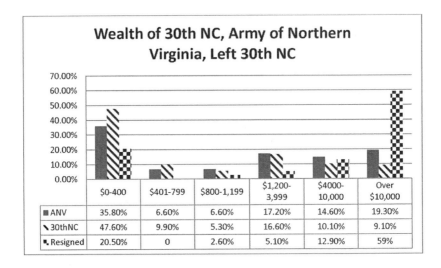

Figure 5. Wealth by Percentages

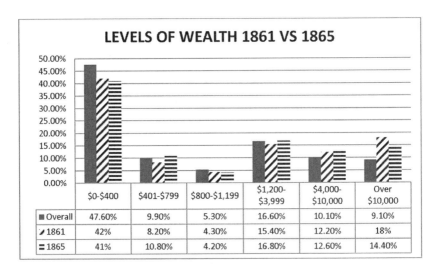

Figure 6. Wealth Over Time

participation as a percentage of the 30th North Carolina dropped by 20 percent (from 18 percent to 14.4 percent) from 1861 to 1865.

Research needs to be done on more regiments before the question of big men versus little men can be truly answered. For the 30th, the answer is more nuanced. It would seem that many big men were willing to volunteer in the first burst of adrenaline of 1861, though perhaps fewer than Glatthaar and Sheehan-Dean have claimed. As the war progressed, however, they tended to drop out and withdraw. We should say it was a big man's war and a little man's fight with the participation of some big men.

There are a few other interesting statistics about the men of the 30th North Carolina that can be gleaned from census records. First, brothers often enlisted together or younger brothers followed older brothers into the same company. Many family links are present. There were four father-son pairs in the unit and two sets of twins. Sixty-six other sets of brothers were present, including six sets of three brothers,[23] one of four brothers and another of five brothers.

Race

Perhaps the most surprising thing found in the 1860 census records is that there seems to have been five men of color in the regiment: James B. Morgan,[24] Thomas Morgan[25] and William Grey Morgan[26] (three sons of Wills Morgan of Edgecombe County); Duncan Goins[27] and Edward Goins[28] of Chatham County.

It is not the number of men of color that surprises. It is that there were any at all. No mention was made in any archival documents that these men were of color. The records are exactly like those of their white fellow soldiers. North Carolina law specified that only white men could volunteer. Yet, the five men were members. This flies in the face of recent scholarship which insists there were no men of color who served in the Confederate Army.[29] When I first saw Duncan Goins called mulatto, my reaction was to assume I had found the wrong man. After investigating the men in depth, I can only conclude that they were exactly what they seem. The controversial nature of men of color requires more than a passing mention.

Duncan and Edward Goins appear in both the 1850 and 1860 census returns as a part of the household of their father, William Goins. In 1850, William is called a miller. In 1860, he is a carpenter with $150 in personal property. The entire family is called mulatto in both records.[30]

James B. Thomas and William Grey Morgan are in the household of their father Wells (or Wills) Morgan in 1860. The adults are laborers with no property. All are called mulatto. None of the family can be located with certainty in other records.[31]

There are, of course, other possible interpretations of the data. Census takers tended to refer to men with Native American ancestry as mulatto. However, in Chatham County, where the Goins brothers lived, there were few if any traces of Native Americans. Perhaps the men had darker complexions and were not known personally to the census taker who arbitrarily chose to list them as mulatto. One could think of many reasons why men might be called mulatto other than being free men of color. Keri Merritt, on the other hand, presents very strong evidence on sexual and social mixing of poor whites and slaves as well as free people of color.[32] The historian must, in the end, write history based on the documents and not what he thinks the documents should say. Therefore, we will state our belief that the five volunteers were free men of color.

Literacy

We can determine an approximate level of literacy. Standard sources indicate that among whites in 1850, 25 percent of males were illiterate. Including women gives a number of 29 percent.[33] By 1860, illiteracy among men had dropped to around 20 percent. The 1860 census noted illiteracy. During the war most soldiers were required from time to time to sign receipts for pay or supplies, and when such documents were available to archivists assembling Personal Jackets it was noted if a man signed with "His Mark." While we cannot be certain that surviving documents present a true picture, it would seem to be reasonable. Two hundred and sixty-five men (17.6 percent) could not sign their names. They are distributed fairly evenly across the regiment: Company A 30; Company B 18; Company C 32; Company D 39; Company E 31; Company F 37; Company G 20; Company H 20; Company I 26; Company K 12.

Physical Appearance

We can make some estimates about physical appearance. Men captured by the Union Army were eventually freed, either paroled during the war, or if they swore not to rebel again, when the war was over. They were normally described on the document. Also men who were discharged from the regiment for any reason were described. In both cases descriptions included height, age, complexion, hair color and eye color. Two hundred and fifteen men can be so described from the documents in Personal Jackets. There is no reason to assume that this sample is not fairly random across the regiment.

The height of 30th North Carolina men was exactly what you would expect. Most historians now believe that the average height of an American soldier in the Revolutionary War was about 5'8", nearly two inches taller than the typical British soldier. The average size of a Civil War soldier is usually given as 5'8". The average 30th North Carolina soldier was slightly taller than 5'8¾" (5.7376 in decimal feet and inches). The smallest man was 4'8"[34] and the tallest was 6'4".[35] The median height was 5'9⅛" and the most common height was 5'10" (Figure 7).

Geographical Origins

It is not surprising that the overwhelming majority of the members of the 30th North Carolina were from North Carolina. However,

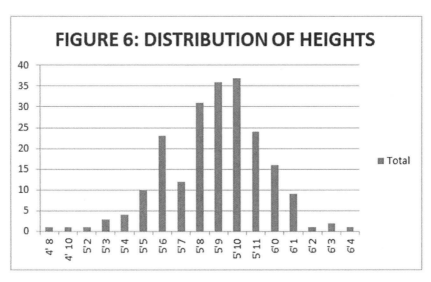

Figure 7. Distribution of Heights

there were four men from Alabama, one from England,[36] one from Gibraltar, three from Ireland, one from Massachusetts, one from New York, one from Philadelphia, six from South Carolina, 11 from Virginia and 11 unknown place of origin.

Ages

War is carried out by young men. We have found ages at enlistment for 99.9 percent (1,490) of the men of the 30th. Eighteen-year-olds provided the largest number of recruits, 176 (11.9 percent) followed by 19- and 20-year-olds with 103 (6.9 percent) each. The spread of ages was, however, vast. The youngest man, or rather boy, was Walter S. Turner of Company I, at 13 years old. Private Turner has already been cited as the shortest man in the regiment. The oldest man was 58-year-old Nathan Marlow, who was paid to be a substitute in Company F.[37] At the extremes, six boys of age 15, 24 of age 16, and 71 of age 17 joined along with 126 men in their 40s and 12 men in their 50s.

The average age of recruits varied considerably by year. In 1861, the average recruit was 24 years old. In 1862, when the first draft was held he was 25.34 years old. In 1863 under intense conscription, including older men, the average age of an enlistee was 33.22 years. In 1864 when the typical enlistee was newly 18, the average age fell to 19.69 years old. The older men had been forced in already but only men just turning 18 were available. There were no enlistments in 1865.

Given the young age of many of those enlisting in the 30th, it is not surprising that only a minority lived in independent households. From the 1860 census schedule we can determine the household status of 855 men. Over 63 percent of the men were not head of their own households. These 540 included: 439 children; 10 boarders; one apprentice; seven brothers or sons-in-law; six grandsons; one nephew; two step-sons; 22 brothers; 48 employees including hired hands and laborers; one business partner; and three who were relatives but the exact relationship is unclear. The very high number of dependent recruits reinforces the generally low economic status of most recruits.

Married men made up 31 percent (266) of the men while 6 percent (52) were bachelors living alone. In 1860, only 36 (4.2 percent) of the married men had no children; 50 had one child; 45 had two children; 43 had three children; 41 had four children; 22 had five children; 11 had six children; six had seven children; four had eight children; and one man, Alfred J. Morris, had nine children.[38] This compares with 39.3 percent married among infantry in the Army of Northern Virginia, 83.2 percent of whom had children.[39]

The men of the 30th North Carolina display enormous variation in wealth, age, education and other criteria. Some of the differences, as we will see in Chapter 8, were of crucial importance. They had much to do with the survivability of each man.

6

Attitudes Concerning
the War, Slavery
and Religion

In this chapter, we pursue that most ephemeral and illusive topic: ideas and beliefs. What did the men of the 30th North Carolina think and believe about the war, slavery and religion? Members of the regiment often expressed their views in letters and diaries. Unlike letters from later wars, there was no censor present to review and control what information was sent home. Opinions were expressed fully and unapologetically. The men on occasion claimed they reflected widespread opinions. More often they expressed their personal fears, frustrations and hopes to wives and brothers.

> "[T]he men have become very blood thirsty."
> —Louis McLeod

The question of why Confederate soldiers fought has evolved considerably in recent years. The older view was, while planters and the rich clearly saw the war as one to preserve slavery, poor men were motivated to fight for different reasons. They fought to protect their states and homes from invasion or to prove themselves.[1]

Contemporary historians have tended to discount the older view and pose different motivations. The most convincing argument is made by James McPherson.[2] He wrote that both Confederate and Union soldiers were motivated by the same things just from different angles.

The initial burst of volunteers came from what the French call *rage militaire*, patriotic furor to save the homeland, earn glory by being a man and doing one's duty. The reality of warfare ended eagerness for battle. Duty and proving your manhood continued to motivate.

As the war intensified and continued, what motivated the men, McPherson believed, was ideology and, above all, the formation of a band of brothers. Men fought not to let down their brothers and out of increased hatred of the enemy.

McPherson is, I believe, very close to the truth. The only shortcomings are his examples are taken largely from officers and, as he himself says, North Carolina was perhaps something of an anomaly. He notes, for example, that 84 percent of South Carolina soldiers wrote patriotic statements in letters as opposed to only 46 percent of North Carolina soldiers. The one area where I believe he was clearly wrong was in stating that men did not enlist for the money.[3] It was, he believed, simply too small to matter.

Colin Woodward insists the single overwhelming motivation for volunteers was to preserve slavery. "Whether or not men owned African Americans, Confederate soldiers believed that slavery was an economically beneficial, divinely ordained institution that maintained a racially structured social order in the [S]outh."[4] He is convinced the percentage of soldiers owning slaves or intimately involved with slavery was very large. Southerners in general and Confederate soldiers particularly found the threat of abolition far more threatening than class differences. One indication of this view to Woodward is the frequent comparisons soldiers made between themselves and blacks.[5]

Many of Woodward's citations are from the deep South and Virginia. North Carolina is not strongly represented. That perhaps skews his view and makes him less valuable when considering North Carolina soldiers. In all the correspondence from the 30th North Carolina, there is no general discussion of slavery, nor is there any comparison of soldiers with slaves. Nor, as noted above, was the percentage of men who owned slaves particularly high.

There is no question that slavery was the driving force behind the Civil War. There is also little doubt that few white Southerners, save in the mountains perhaps, were not in some way connected to the institution. In addition, we must believe that those men, like nearly all white Americans in 1860, viewed African Americans as inferior people, perhaps even divinely intended as servants and slaves. However, those assumptions do not automatically translate into individual motivation to go to war, especially of poor men.

Sheehan-Dean has addressed motivation in a very different way. He sees early and strong Confederate nationalism as the motivating force behind volunteers. "Most white Virginians transferred their national loyalties to the Confederacy with surprising ease."[6] Furthermore he believes that this "nationalism" continued to motivate Virginians until near the end of 1864 when the cause became hopeless. He offers considerable evidence from letters and newspapers for this belief. He explains this near instantaneous shift in Virginian loyalties in terms of family values and the early occupation of much of the state by Union forces. His argument of Virginia devotion to the Confederacy is convincing, but not his explanation for it. The most likely reason that Virginians might have been fully convinced and loyal Confederates was that from the moment of secession Virginia became nearly synonymous with the Confederacy. Richmond was the capital of both Virginia and the Confederacy; the leading generals were Virginians; Virginia was invaded very early and a great number of major battles were fought there. Virginia and the Confederacy were the same. To argue that Virginians were motivated by loyalty to the Confederacy is the same as saying they were motivated by loyalty to Virginia. This was decidedly not the case for North Carolinians who remained determined to defend their state but showed little enthusiasm for the Confederacy, or one might add at times for Virginia.

The question here is what motivated the men of the 30th North Carolina? No doubt there were some who were desperate to maintain slavery. There may have been some who were Southern patriots and felt some Confederate nationalism. However, neither is mentioned or implied in letters or diaries. What the documents do suggest among initial volunteers is a belief that North Carolina had every right to secede, even if it was unwise, and the reaction of the Union was tantamount to armed invasion. There was much talk about the need to defend their homes, to defend North Carolina.

The men of the 30th seem to reflect much of what McPherson wrote about motivation. They were outraged at the prospect of an invasion of North Carolina. They were eager to "do their duty." The letters of Louis McLeod touch on these two motivations. Judging from his wife Eliza's letters, the couple must have discussed the idea of

McLeod's duty. In early 1862, Eliza pleads with Louis to get out of the army. "Louis i think twelv monts wil bee dooing your duty and then come home and let alters [others] take your place. We want to live and hav something as wel as every body else and we cant doo it and you gone all or the time."[7]

By June 1862 for McLeod at least, the initial *rage militaire* had faded. Not, however, for many of the men. McLeod describes how the men all shouted and yelled as they left for Virginia and battle. He refers to them as "fools all hollering."[8] He did, however, still do his duty and dragged himself out of a sick bed to follow the regiment to the battle.

After the initial burst of volunteers, there was a second motivation in the winter of 1861–1862. When it began to look as though men might have to go because of conscription, some grudgingly volunteered to be with friends and family while they could pick their company and regiment. Those in the army urged friends to do the right thing and not hang back and be forced in.

A third motivation for joining the army was money. James McPherson was wrong on this matter. Kenneth Noe has superbly argued that one reason later Confederates joined was for the bounty and the pay.[9] Men, and not just poor men, took the bounty to join, or to extend; they accepted money to substitute for someone else; they eagerly awaited pay day. This was true in 1861 and even later. Not all were motivated by high ideals or national loyalties. We already cited Louis McLeod who remarked to his wife that many men wanted the $50 or $100. It was, he said, more than a heap of them can make in a year. The recent writing of William Marvel makes it clear that a great many Union soldiers were also primarily motivated by money, not high principle.[10]

There is one more likely reason many of the men volunteered. It would be a short, easy war and young men very often have a tendency to love a good fight. The desire to prove your manhood and emerge from the test of battle a hero no doubt motivated many.[11] When friends and relatives are announcing their decision to march off and win the day, the desire to show bravery and be a hero surely brought more than a few to volunteer.

It is unlikely that any of the initial motivations, including seeing the Union Army as invaders, was in itself sufficient to create the psychological changes necessary to convert recruits into "blood thirsty" soldiers. Historical studies of the ways in which the enemy is portrayed in all modern wars repeat the same theme: the enemy must be seen as barely human or, if human, utterly depraved. The enemy is not just capable of doing evil, he is certain to do so. When Colonel Parker addressed the men in May 1862, he referred to the Union soldiers as "those devils." He warned the men what the Yankees would do to women, wives, sisters, daughters if they were permitted to succeed. The reports about early battles in North Carolina that circulated through North Carolina and the army portrayed the Union soldiers as creatures who were without mercy, who jeered and ridiculed Carolinians.[12] The example was held up often of how Mrs. Sanders was treated by the Yankee captain. The story she told, and that was repeated with embellishment no doubt, was that the Yankee captain rode his horse up to the house, shook his sword over her head and ordered her to given up all her property and food.[13] Perhaps he did and perhaps in reality the man was the epitome of politeness. Regardless, the story was told and retold to show the cruelty of Union soldiers. Men have a need to see the enemy as evil and not fully human. How else could you be eager to kill men that two years before had been your fellow citizens? When James L. Green was conscripted in 1863, he traveled to Raleigh by way of Salisbury where he saw Union prisoners in the POW camp there. He wrote home, "I wanted my gun to shoot them."[14] When Louis McLeod described to his wife the first known kill of his company he compared it to dropping a squirrel off a tree.[15]

Ardrey noted in his diary that three members of his company, Bill Williamson,[16] Dearmond[17] and Bently[18] were captured by the Union Army at Antietam. They were quickly paroled by the Yankees, who to Ardrey's surprise treated them "remarkable well."[19] They returned with trinkets and pure coffee. Evidently it was still possible this early in the war to see Yankees as less than devils.

If volunteers came to see the Yankees as devils, this was emphatically not true of many conscripts.[20] Many, perhaps most, conscripts were reluctant soldiers and often opposed to the war. A standard refrain given by conscripts, and even some volunteers captured by the Union from 1863 on, was they had been conscripted against their will. Their fondest desire was to once again be a loyal supporter of the United States. These protestations must, of course, be viewed with some skepticism since at least some of them were surely uttered hoping to secure better treatment or even release from Union prison. The 18 men who volunteered to join the United States Army made a stronger statement of Union partisanship. Some of the stories told of unwillingness to serve in the Confederate Army are emotional and heart-wrenching.

John W. Bray was captured 8 May 1864 at Spotsylvania Court House. He was conscripted 1 July 1862 but hid "in the woods" at home until he was captured on 2 December 1863. He was taken to the regiment and kept under close guard until the battle of Spotsylvania when he deserted to the Union. He told his captors that he wanted to take the oath of loyalty and go to Indiana.[21] H.B. Rose, Company H, insisted he was conscripted in March 1863, was always opposed to the war and that he had two bothers in the 146th New York Regiment. All his friends were in the north.[22]

Thomas Brinkly was conscripted 1 July 1863 and assigned to Company B. He reached the bivouac of the regiment in Orange County, Virginia, by December 1863, but never reported to the company. Once his escorts released him, he disappeared and, therefore, deserted even before he was a real member of the regiment.

The two brothers Ralph and William Currin of Granville County present a very interesting case. They both enlisted on 1 May 1862 probably as a result of the draft. William was admitted to the Wilmington Hospital in June with "fever." Upon his release both brothers were furloughed but at the end of the furloughs they deserted and for 18 months were "lurking in the woods in Granville County." They returned to duty in December 1863 perhaps out of health concerns. William was at once admitted to Wilmington Hospital, again for "fever," and Ralph evidently had severe mental problems for he was admitted to a hospital in Raleigh. In January 1864, Ralph was transferred to Charlottesville suffering from "mania." On 6 February 1864, he was transferred to Richmond General Hospital #1 with "acute mania," then given a 60-day furlough. He never returned to duty. William remained with Company G until late March or early April 1865. He was not present at Appomattox but was paroled on 14 April 1865.[23]

John L. Miller told his captors that if he were freed he would go to Illinois. "I'd like to go home and see my friends as well as anybody, but am not willing to help the southern Confederacy. It is against my principles." He would be willing to join the Union Army if he knew he would be treated like any other soldier if taken prisoner.[24]

There were, of course, men who used the bounty system as a way to make money and avoid as much danger as possible. They were referred to often as "bounty jumpers," men who signed up with a unit and deserted as soon as they received the bounty. A man might do this several times in succession given the lack of central record-keeping. Alfred Black, Company H, may have been one. He seems to have been a regular member through June 1862 as he was wounded at Gaines Mill. Having seen enough, Private Black went AWOL around 1 September 1862 and remained so through the end of 1863. However, during those 14 months, he volunteered for two other units, the 36th North Carolina Infantry and the 13th North Carolina Light Artillery, presumably for the bounty. He returned to the 30th in late February 1864. He was lightly wounded and was captured or deserted at Spotsylvania. Black embellished the story to his captors claiming he was a veteran of the Mexican War and had served five years in the U.S. Artillery; had been seized in Fayetteville and forced into the army; he voluntarily gave up to a Zouave Regiment during the battle.[25]

Slavery

> "Tell him to give the rascal a good whipping if he runs off again."
> —John B. Witherspoon

> "Tell Henry and Ary and Nelse I think of them very oftin...."
> —Louis McLeod

In the Confederacy, enslaved people made up 40 percent of the population and free people of color another 2 percent. Moore County, North Carolina, the home of most of the men of Company H, was not a large slave-owning place.[26] Roughly one-quarter of the free households, 468, owned slaves. However, 294 of those consisted of one to four slaves. The largest slave owner was R.C. Colter who was superintendent of construction for the Western Railroad being built to the Egypt coal mine. His 39 slaves and 11 white men who boarded with lilm were all being used to build the railroad. Other companies of the 30th came from areas with larger plantations.

There were certainly rich men who went to war to protect slavery, but the institution itself was not a topic of discussion in letters or diaries. Doubtless the overwhelming majority of the men were at least passive supporters of slavery. It is highly unlikely that any were in favor of abolition or emancipation. There are, however, many references about individual slaves. These comments let us draw inferences on attitudes towards slavery and men of color generally.

Attitudes towards slaves tended to correlate with economic status: hardly surprising. Letters from men who owned a substantial number of slaves reflected a more impersonal feeling about enslaved people. While individuals are often mentioned by name, letters were primarily concerned with maintaining discipline and efficient work. John G. Witherspoon offers a perfect example. He owned only six slaves in 1860 but his substantial real estate and personal property, as well as the high literacy of his letters, indicate a young man from a very well-to-do family. His attitudes, businesslike and hard, certainly reflect high status. His wife Hassie must have complained that the slaves were giving trouble and not behaving in the absence of the master. Witherspoon was very angry—"makes me boil"—and while he wrote that it was time for the Negroes to have their shoes for the winter, he wrote that he would "get a man to attend to my business that will discipline those negroes if that is the way they are going to conduct themselves."[27] A year and a half later, Witherspoon was still concerned about the behavior of his slaves. He had managed to get home on leave and must have spent a good deal of time threatening the slaves. "Josh made me some very fair promises if I would not sell him. If he don't please you tell him he can't live with you. I am determined to sell him off if he don't please us."[28]

What of men who owned few slaves? The typical North Carolina slave owner was a farmer who owned one, two or three enslaved people. These slaves lived much closer to the whites than did those on larger plantations. The letters between Louis McLeod and his wife are especially interesting here. They owned three slaves. In 1860, Henry was 58, Nelsie (or Nellee, or Nelce) was a 40-year-old woman and Arry was a 10-year-old boy.[29] What we don't know about these three people is larger than what we do know. What was their relationship to each other? In short, were they a family? Was Arry a child of Nelsie or of both? Even limiting ourselves to purely economic aspects we know little. How did they come to be living on the McLeod farm? McLeod was largely estranged from his father so did not inherit slaves or other property. Did they come from Eliza Walker McLeod's inheritance? Were they purchased together or singly? We will never know. Late in the 19th century, the Moore County court house burned and the records which would have answered those questions perished. We can only look at the letters for detail.

In a letter dated 3 November, McLeod sends his best love and respects to Henry, Arry and Nelsie along with the children, a young couple living with his family, Eliza's sister-in-law from an earlier marriage who lived with them and the three dogs. It should be noted that the word love was used in the sense of regards and thoughts. Eliza sends her "best love" to the captain and friends and cousins in Company H—never to her husband. On 24 November, Eliza said the children said howdy and "Nelee said I most rite to you that he could plow and he was worken mity hard to make you biskit to eat when you com home."[30] On 1 December 1861, Henry and Arry and Nelee say they want McLeod to come home for Christmas. In a letter of 9 February 1862, "Nelce sade to tel you he was wel and harty."[31]

To take only two more examples. As the regiment was on the verge of leaving for Virginia, McLeod wrote, "Tell Henry and Ary and Nelse I think of them verry oftin and I want them to think where I am and I want them to try and make a plenty to eat. Best respects to children."[32] One of the most intriguing messages is from Eliza. Evidently, McLeod had heaped much praise on Nelse and had suggested in a letter that has not survived—probably in jest—that Nelse should be the overseer on the plantation. "Henry and ary an nelee sends howdy ... nelee was mity well pleased at what you rote. Bragg [McLeod's 12-year-old son] sade nelee wondent bee over ser over him."[33]

There is no reason to think that the attitudes reflected by Louis and Eliza McLeod were atypical. Sergeant A.F. Harrington's nephew J.K.P. Harrington in a letter home requested that Africa, Bill and Wes write him. He would like to receive their letters and was sure that they would have something interesting to say.[34] Did they do so? Letters written to J.K.P. Harrington have not survived so we don't know. It is probable that Henry, Nelee and Arry could not write else they would have added a note to some of the letters. Africa could write. There is a letter he wrote to his master John Harrington in 1864 when he was working on fortifications in Fayetteville, North Carolina.

William Ardrey noted that he entrusted a crucial letter to his sweetheart written at home on leave to George, "the trusty slave." George did not disappoint and returned with good news.[35]

What are we to infer from this information? Certainly not that the McLeods, Harringtons or anyone else in the 30th North Carolina was opposed to slavery or saw men of color as the equals of whites. Hardly any white man in 1860, in any part of the United States, saw any man of color as his intellectual equal. Individuals, however, were often held with deep respect and affections by whites. This is hardly shocking. We often see those close to us as better than the average. It is also not shocking that individual men of color, including slaves, would have returned that affection since we all tend to respond to kindness and respect with gratitude and reciprocity; in difficult, even terrible situations, we accommodate and rationalize.

Several other indications of this kind of individual affection and conditional respect are evident in letters of the 30th North Carolina. Lieutenant-Colonel Sillers' letters home to his sister often mention with affection his servant Ransome. He related with evident approval that in the town of Gettysburg, Ransome "fell in with some pllaging soldiers ... and got some things for his mother."[36] Enslaved men like Ransome evidently moved about the country, in and out of the war zone, with no difficulty. In the same letter of 7 August, Sillers said he would like to send Ransome home for a while to find out who was causing trouble among the field slaves but he could not spare him.[37] No indication was given about what kind of "trouble" was going on in the slave quarters, but Sillers expected that Ransome's total loyalty was with him rather than his fellow enslaved men. After Sillers was killed at Kelly's Ford in November 1863 Ransome, according to Sillers' friend G.F. Williams, nearly "grieved himself to death."[38] Williams sent Ransome home with Sillers' watch and pocketbook and $360. Ransome was going to go by Richmond and "get some things." Williams asked that Ransome be sent back so that he could take Sillers' horse to North Carolina. One assumes that Ransome had a letter explaining to authorities who he was and why he was traveling alone, but there seems to have been no thought that it was not proper nor that Ransome would not carry out his duty explicitly.

Colonel Parker's farm manager was drafted and, rather than try and get the man exempt, Parker felt that it was proper that he should serve. He advised his wife to put one of the slaves, Hilliard, in charge of the plantation.[39]

Men of Color in the Regiment

One of the unanswerable questions is how were the six men of color treated by their companies and by the regiment. James B., Thomas and William Grey Morgan (three sons of Wills Morgan of Edgecombe County); John R. Jones of Halifax County and Duncan and Edwards Goins of Chatham County were all listed in the 1860 census as free mulattos. The men were all illiterate and served loyally as members of the 30th. Three of them were wounded, two were captured and one died. There are no indications in the records of the 30th that these men were of color. They seem to have been treated and accepted as full and equal members of the regiment.

There were other men of color attached to the regiment as cooks and workers. William Ardrey mentions in his diary that early in January 1864 two men returned from furlough home. One of them was the cook Henry Phillips,[40] a free-born colored man.[41] Colonel Parker employed a free mulatto, Dick Hicks, as cook. The colonel wrote to his wife early in 1864 that rations were so short that they only ate twice a day but that "Dick Hicks[42] is a good cook. He can make a better biscuit than any woman; he cooks my peas well done for me too."[43]

Religion

> "I do not omit to pray, or rather I do not neglect prayer entirely; but I do not pray as often and as fervently as I should."
> —William Sillers, March 1863

It must be assumed that all of the men of the 30th North Carolina were at least passive believers in God. It would have been a remarkable man in 1860 who was a non-believer. Nevertheless, early in the war there were vast differences in the level and intensity of belief. We do not know if there were men in the 30th whose Presbyterian belief in predestination could match that of Thomas Jackson or D.H. Hill who insisted they were as safe on a battlefield as in a parlor since God had already determined when they would die. It is certain many of the officers were devout men who devoted a considerable time to prayer and worship. William Sillers must have been one. He admitted in one letter, "I do not omit to pray, or rather I do not neglect prayer entirely; but I do not pray as often and as fervently, as I should."[44]

Colonel Parker did his part to foster religious devotion. Occasionally he proclaimed "days of fasting and thanksgiving." The colonel did not care for the chaplain and thought him "altogether too sanctimonious, uses too many extravagant expressions."[45] Parker was evidently in some turmoil about his faith. He wrote to his wife that he had much anguish and feared that somehow he was "unworthy of Christianity."[46]

What we can see about attitudes toward religion among the ranks and less-educated men would indicate considerable indifference before 1863.[47] Little is said about God, prayer and devotions. However, if Eliza McLeod is a representative example, their wives were very concerned with God's approval. She often wrote about her fear that God had abandoned the South. The war was brought on by "sin and pride." She often entreated Louis not to forget his God and depend on God's help. McLeod, on the other hand, never expressed similar beliefs to Eliza.

When war goes badly, when men fear loss and death, they often turn in desperation to religion hoping that God will turn the tide and save them. In the fall of 1863, this was true of the 30th North Carolina along with much of the Confederate Army. It was clear to the men of the regiment after the retreat from Gettysburg that things were going very badly for the South. Increased desertions are one indication of this. Early in September, 10 men in Ewell's corps were shot for desertion.[48] Men now feared that failure was possible, and they might have "to live under old Abe."[49] Perhaps it was that despair that led to a great religious revival in the entire brigade in September of 1863.[50]

The beginnings of this awakening may have been before June. Chaplain Betts preached to a large crowd on Sunday, 24 May at Hamilton's Crossing, Virginia. Several men professed their faith and were baptized in the river.[51] Rufus Stallings commented to his future wife that even before Gettysburg there was a big upturn in religion. Lots of boys "joined the church." He and Forbes were baptized the third Sunday of June.[52] On 22 August all duties were suspended and a "fast-day" proclaimed. According to William Sillers, many observed the day "but many paid no respect to it."[53]

By September the regiment was much in the throes of religious revival. A.F. Harrington described it this way, "We has a big meeting here[.] Preching every day & night[.] thare is a grate revival in our Brigade[.] Thare is a grate change in the Army at this time[.] I hardly ever here a man use any profane language without he is some man that drives a wagon or some one that never has bin in danger of ball."[54]

William Ardrey was much impressed with the revival. Instead of the few hundred men who had been religious before now there were two thousand attending service every night with two hundred penitents every night. There was preaching day and night under a large brush arbor made by the soldiers surrounded by torch lights at night.[55] The intensity kept up from the end of August until 14 September when marching orders were received.

J.W. Bone remembered that many men were more religious.[56] While the nature of the Bone memoir is such that exact dates cannot be assigned, he writes of the period in late 1863 that there were chapels built, services and revivals were common and many men "made profession" and took to religion. It is unclear how long this great revival lasted, but all indications are that it faded away as the army entered the misery of early 1864. Of course, both armies insisted God supported them. The Almighty evidently chose to back the larger and better equipped Union Army.

7

Battle-Related Casualties

"I am tired and sick of war. Its glory is all moonshine.
It is only those who have neither fired a shot nor heard
the shrieks and groans of the wounded, who cry aloud
for blood, for vengeance, for desolation. War is hell."
—William Tecumseh Sherman

For nine months, the men of the 30th North Carolina cried aloud for blood, for vengeance. They wrote often of their great desire to meet the enemy in the field and slaughter them and drive those not dead out of North Carolina. In late June 1862, they at last met the enemy, but they met him in Virginia not North Carolina.

For the 30th North Carolinians, the Civil War truly began in June 1862. In a desperate move to save Richmond from capture by McClellan and Union forces, the Confederacy brought every regiment possible to Virginia. The 30th North Carolina was among them.

When Louis McLeod arrived at Richmond, he wrote home in astonishment at the number of soldiers assembled. "Of all the men I ever saw we have got them here. The hole face of the land is covered with men and horses and wagons. The land is in a perfect wirk with them."[1] According to rumor in the camp, or a Richmond newspaper, there were 230,000 Southerners there ready to fall on the Union forces.[2] The actual number, including Jackson's division still in the Shenandoah, was closer to 80,000 or 90,000 and always outnumbered by Union forces.[3]

By the end of their first week in Virginia, the men of the 30th North Carolina had not only been blooded, they had been given a brutal initiation into the reality of war. The hell would last nearly three years. From June 1862 through early April 1865, the 30th North Carolina marched, fought skirmishes and pitched battles. They suffered extreme cold without proper clothing. When not marching or fighting, the regiment was attacked by disease, near famine and increasing disillusionment with the war. During its active duty, the 30th would suffer 90 percent attrition—1,506 men and officers were enrolled and only 153 surrendered on 9 April 1865. Obviously not all of the 90 percent died or were captured, though many did suffer those fates. Over the course of three years increasing numbers of men deserted, or went AWOL. Some transferred to other units; some never returned from furloughs. Many finished the war in hospitals. Some were dismissed from the service on grounds of being unfit for duty because of wounds or disease. In this chapter we will give a cursory description of the battle history of the regiment and broadly analyze casualties suffered by the 30th.

On to Virginia

> *"we got orders to move to Virginia ... at nine that knight the train blew a long whissle and the regiment went with the train and the fools all hollering ... but that is the case with every regiment that goes by hear."*
> —Louis McLeod, 15 June 1862

The volunteers who joined the 30th North Carolina in 1861 did so, they believed, to defend the state against invasion. As we have seen, such an invasion did take place in 1862, but the men of the 30th North Carolina never fired a single shot in their own state except in training. By the early summer of 1862, the danger to the Confederacy was in Virginia where McClellan was slowly moving up the peninsula toward Richmond with a force that consistently outnumbered the defenders. The 30th would spend the rest of the war in Virginia, Maryland and Pennsylvania. It would never fight one day in North Carolina.

The main part of the 30th North Carolina left Wilmington on 13 June and arrived at Petersburg on 16 June 1862. However, a significant number had stayed behind. From Company H alone 21 men including Lieutenant Louis McLeod remained in quarters, too sick to travel, and many others were hospitalized.[4] On 18 June, McLeod furloughed 14 men home, and he and six others boarded a train for Richmond, arriving on the 19th when they joined the regiment in camp near Richmond just off the Williamsburg Road. Before leaving Wilmington, the regiment counted 811 men present or accounted for. If Company H was typical of the level of sickness, the actual number camping near Richmond could have been as low as 600 or 650 and certainly was not more than 700 men and officers.

The regiment suffered its first wounded and counted its first kill on the first day it was put on picket duty, Saturday, 21 June.[5] The men were loosely deployed next to a deep swamp. The other side of the swamp was held by the Union Army which fired artillery and grape over and through the swamp. No one was killed, but three men were wounded. Later in the day, 20 men were sent into the swamp as skirmishers. Denis Carr[6] of Company H told his company mates that he crept into the swamp, set himself up and soon saw a Yankee, gun slung, climbing a tree. Carr laid his gun against a sapling and dropped the Yankee off "like a squirrel, dead as Hector."[7]

One of the first casualties was Eugene Grissom, Captain Company D. Grissom was 35 when he signed up in August 1861. On 22 June 1862, he was wounded in a skirmish. The wound fractured one clavicle, causing partial paralysis of shoulder and arm. He was given wounded leave and while home was elected to the North Carolina House of Commons. He requested a 90-day leave to serve but was apparently refused. In February 1863, he resigned from the army as disabled.

The nature of the war in the peninsula had changed on 1 June. The original commander of Confederate forces was Joseph Johnston who was the highest ranking officer to leave the U.S. Army for the Confederacy. With very limited forces, Johnston had impeded the Union advance by taking advantage of McClellan's excessive cautiousness. By late May, troops were arriving daily and Johnston felt comfortable in taking the offensive. Johnston's plans for what became known as the Battle of Seven Pines fell apart almost before the battle began. In addition, he was seriously wounded and unable to continue in command. On 1 June 1862, Robert E. Lee took field command of the army.

General Lee believed he had a sufficient number of troops to destroy McClellan rather than just impede his advance. Lee devised a bold plan that brought Thomas Jackson on a rapid, unexpected move from the Shenandoah Valley, combined with seizing crucial bridges over the Chickahominy River in order to move the divisions of the two Hills and Longstreet into a position to wipe out Union forces that had been isolated on the north side of the river. Lee believed that the destruction of that part of the Union Army would so panic McClellan that he would flee back down the peninsula and perhaps the entire Union Army could be destroyed in the confusion. What resulted was the Seven Days Campaign, in which four pitched battles were fought. The 30th as part of D.H. Hill's division was much involved in the second and fourth battles.

The second battle was Gaines Mill on 28 June. It was a Confederate victory but not as decisive as planned because Jackson did not arrive when promised and when he did arrive, strangely, did not commit to battle. For the first time, the 30th North Carolina found itself in the thick of battle, and it was a brutal introduction to war: 17 killed, six died of wounds and 52 wounded.

There was a lull in battle because rather than force the crossing of the Chickahominy, Jackson dithered and rebuilt a bridge destroyed by retreating federals. On 30 June, the bridge was completed and Jackson's corps, which included his brother-in-law D.H. Hill's division, crossed the river and quickly went into battle at White Oak Bridge. Again the battle was not decisive, but McClellan retreated and it seemed another victory for the South. The 30th was held in reserve and did not enter the fight.

Lee's plan was in tatters but McClellan was retreating, much to the disgust of his own generals. Lee saw one last chance to achieve the great victory he sought when Union forces occupied a small plateau called Malvern Hill. D.H. Hill personally reconnoitered the approach. When Lee called his commanders together on 30 June, Hill spoke strongly against attacking. The Union was dug in and had placed a great deal of artillery in such a way that a frontal attack seemed suicidal. Lee seems never to have fully decided what to do, and his lack of direction led to a blundering, piecemeal attack on Malvern Hill on 1 July 1862. The attack was as disastrous as Hill had predicted, and his division which participated fully was terribly wounded and never managed to reach the Union forces. The 30th suffered 20 killed, 17 dead of wounds and 90 wounded at Malvern Hill, a terrible toll.[8]

Lee was credited with saving Richmond and the Confederacy. The reality was that Richmond was saved by McClellan's refusal to commit his full force to battle. Had he done so, the far weaker Southern forces could have been swept aside and the war perhaps ended. Instead

Jefferson Davis, Robert E. Lee and other leaders of the Confederacy were left with the illusion that victory and independence were within their grasp if they only persevered. It would be men like those of the 30th North Carolina who would pay the price for this self-delusion (Figure 8).

By the end of July, the 30th North Carolina numbered again around 700 men and officers of which, according to Colonel Parker, about half were hospitalized or sick in camp unable to function. The remainder of the summer, the 30th North Carolina mostly was kept in reserve, avoiding the Battle of Second Manassas. By the beginning of September, a few of the wounded and stragglers had returned, but summer was the peak time for typhoid deaths and dysentery, both of which took their toll and resulted in the regiment dropping to between 575 and 600 men and officers present or accounted for.

On 4 September 1862, the 30th crossed the Potomac for the first

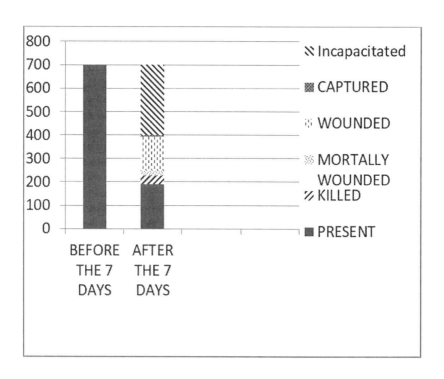

Figure 8. Strength Before and After the Seven Days

73

time to a glorious welcome by those Marylanders who had wanted their state to secede. Leaving Frederick a few days later, the 30th made up the rear guard of Longstreet's column. The men deployed at South Mountain and Fox's Gap but saw little fighting. On 15 September, the regiment was placed on the heights east of Antietam Creek near Sharpsburg, and in the terrible battle on the 17th the regiment held down the right side of the Sunken Road. It is difficult to give an accurate number of men going into the battle. The records show more than 650 as September began. It is, however, certain that many lagged behind and dropped out during the march and the skirmishes leading up to Antietam. Major Sillers, who took command after Colonel Parker was grievously wounded, wrote in his official report that the regiment went into the battle "with about 250 [men] all told." Even though in the thick of battle during this bloodiest day in American history, the 30th North Carolina suffered relatively moderate casualties—eight men were killed and seven died of wounds (2.5 percent dead), 52 (8.6 percent) were wounded and 47 (7.8 percent) were captured (Figure 9).

Retreating back over the Potomac, the 30th spent much of the fall in the Shenandoah as a part of Jackson's "Foot Cavalry" racing up and down the Valley, involved in numerous small battles with Union forces. It ended the year at Fredericksburg where minor casualties were taken from artillery but the unit was never in that bloody battle.

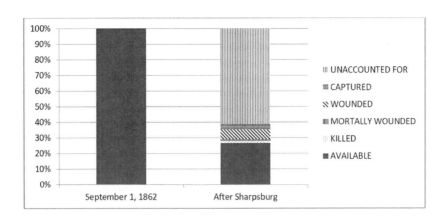

Figure 9. Strength Before and After Antietam (Sharpsburg)

After Fredericksburg, the 30th North Carolina went into camp near Hamilton Crossing, Virginia, where it remained all winter, not moving away until late April 1863. The number of men remained between 500 and 600 during the winter. Many men simply left and went home without leave, and disease continued to kill or put men into hospitals. However, by early 1863 many wounded, furloughed or absent without leave had recovered, well fed at home and began returning to the unit.

Military operations began again in earnest on 1 May 1863 when the roughly 600 men of the 30th North Carolina moved towards Chancellorsville, Virginia. The 30th was again part of Jackson's corps and, thus, part of Jackson's long march to flank the Union Army. The 30th was on the right flank when on 2 May, Jackson's corps fell on the unsuspecting Union troops and routed them. On 3 May, the 30th was involved in several actions and was part of the forces that turned the Union flank. The regiment took several hundred Union prisoners. The 30th North Carolina shared much of the glory of the Confederate victory at Chancellorsville. It paid, however, a very high price: 35 men (5.8 percent) were killed or died of wounds; 74 men (12.3 percent) were wounded.

Pennsylvania

> *"John that day & night was a nuf to kill horses let lone men[.] I never want to go back thare a gain."*
> —A.F. Harrington

In mid–June 1863, the 30th, numbering around 500 men and officers, was part of Ramseur's brigade which was assigned to Rodes's division and 2nd Corps now commanded by Richard Ewell after Jackson's death at Chancellorsville. The brigade was the lead unit returning to the Shenandoah Valley. On 15 June, the brigade led the way across the Potomac—very reluctantly according to William Ardrey—for the second time and crossed into Pennsylvania on 22 June. By the end of the month, the brigade and the 30th North Carolina had reached the furthest north of any Confederate unit, occupying the army barracks at Carlisle, Pennsylvania.[9] By 30 June, the entire force was again marching south and on 1 July arrived at the small town of Gettysburg, Pennsylvania. The 30th was much involved in the fighting on both 1 and 2 July.[10] Some men had dropped out during the march; at least nine deserted, but it was still at about half strength. By 4 July, the defeated Army of Northern Virginia was retreating south, and the 30th made up part of the rear guard until safely back across the Potomac on 14 July. The retreat was brutal. Not only did the 30th have to fight many times, but Union cavalry caught the regimental wagon train insufficiently protected[11] and destroyed or captured much of the train including the Regimental Headquarters' wagon—all supplies very much needed.

Once again, even though the 30th was in the heart of much of the fighting at Gettysburg, its casualties were moderate: nine men (2 percent) were killed or died; 22 (4.5 percent) were wounded and 35 men (7 percent) were captured.

It was very clear to the men of the 30th that they had been in a decisive battle. Sergeant A.F. Harrington wrote his brother John about how the entire experience felt. Much of the letter is worth producing here:

> We are now in Camp one more time after a long march & hard fighting. We marched a bout too months. We went to the old United States Garison in PA. in fifteen miles of the Capital of the State. Pensilvana is a grate cuntry but I tell you the old dutch look sower at us. We got a plenty of something good to eat molasses sugar & coffee & ice & whiskey. Going on done varry well but coming back give us fits. John we had a hard time at Gatysburg. Ramseurs Brigade attacted in front of the town the yankeys was behind a rock fence thare. They give us fits. They poured in one hold volley in to our Regiment but we charged it & taken more prisners than we had men. Louis Wicker[12] was kild ded on the field & we had 10 men wounded. We went rite thrue town & clerd the town out[.] thare we stade all night & all day next day & held the town. A.P. Hill charged the hights & thare we lost men. July the 3 was the gratest cannonading I ever herd. The 4 we fell back to the river and it was so high that we could not cross. We formed a line of battle! ... & staid thare too days till the river fell. The yankeys come on & we would whip them back & then we would trot again. We got a cross the 14 about 1 Oclock at night. It was up to my brest. You may guess how it was with the low ass men. John that was the worst night I ever traveld. The mud was nee deep. Our men loost thare shoes in the mud mitely But we was traveling from the blue ass yanks. Then We came down to front Royal. The yanks got before us in the menassee gap. Thare we fought them. We had marched 30 miles that day But we formed too lines of battle! ... and we was on the second line whare I could see the fighting going on. I was on a mountain whare I could see them

plain. They had three lines & they advanced nice a while till our shels commenst butsting a mong them. They had too fall back. That was sun set then. That night we skedadeld. We traveld all night. John that day & night was a nuf to kill horses let lone men [.] I never want to go back thare a gain [.] ... Our company is all well. The Co is small now we have 25 men officers & all.[13]

William Ardrey described the crossing of the Potomac in similar terms: neck-deep to a low man, waded with their clothes on, rain falling incessantly, the mud nearly knee-deep. Marched the entire night and never rested a single time.[14]

In October 1863, the 30th North Carolina was involved in skirmishes which killed two men and wounded nine. On 7 November, the 30th was ordered to support the 2nd North Carolina Regiment in a minor engagement on the Rappahannock River which turned disastrous for the 30th. The 2nd was retreating at a place called Kelly's Ford and when the 30th moved to support, it too was pinned down by intense fire and advancing troops. Attempts were made to rally the men and get them out of the trap, but many refused to leave what shelter they had found, and in the end much of the 30th was overrun and captured. It went in with about 640 men and had 130 (20 percent) captured, 12 (2 percent) killed and 27 (4.2 percent) wounded.

The 30th spent the winter of 1863–1864 in camp at Orange Court House, Virginia. Aside from some heavy skirmishes, the regiment saw no action until May 1864 when Grant began to move into the Wilderness. On 5 May 1864 the 30th was left back, placed on the extreme left of the Confederate line on the 6th and then held in reserve on the 7th. The 30th was not so fortunate in the days after the Wilderness. Grant was determined never to let up, and the two armies met again at Spotsylvania Court House. For six days, 8–13 May, they fought and skirmished. This time the 30th was in the thick of things. May 1864 was one of the worst months for the 30th. It began the month with approximately 511 men and officers. Casualties, largely at Spotsylvania Court House, were devastating: 41 (8 percent) were killed or died of wounds; seven (1.4 percent) captured; and 49 (9.6 percent) wounded. In addition to battle casualties there were desertions and disease. As a result, during May 1864 the 30th was reduced by 36 percent from 511 to 330.[15]

In June 1864, the 30th, now part of William R. Cox's brigade and Rodes' division, was assigned to Jubal Early's corps. In mid-month the corps moved to Lynchburg to defend that city and when the expected Union attack faded, the corps moved into the Shenandoah Valley. On 6 July, the 30th crossed the Potomac into Maryland for the third time. Early planned to take the war to Lincoln and on 11 July reached Washington, D.C. Reconnaissance made it clear that any attack on Washington would be suicidal, and Early turned his corps back towards Virginia. William Ardrey rejoined the regiment on 21 July 1864 and noted in his diary that there were but three officers and 75 men with the regiment.[16]

The 30th would be involved in several battles in the late summer: Snickers Gap on 18 July, Stephenson Depot on 20 July and Kernstown on 24 July. In August, Philippe Sheridan moved his newly created Army of the Shenandoah into the Valley determined to make Union control permanent. As Sheridan succeeded in his mission, the 30th was involved in frequent skirmishes and small battles. Casualties were never high but the constant attrition took its toll. Even with the return of wounded and detached men, the 30th went into winter quarters in December with less than 300 men present or accounted for.

In 1865, the 30th stayed near its winter quarters until mid–March went it was sent into the trenches defending Petersburg. It remained there until the fall of Petersburg and was involved in the fierce fighting of 25 March in the failed attempt to break the Union siege. Despite being in the thick of things in March and early April, the 30th suffered no killed. However, thirty men died of disease during the first quarter of 1865. As the army retreated west in April 1865, it must have been clear to all that no chance for victory existed. The 30th suffered 62 men captured, or more accurately put, saw 62 of its number find ways to surrender to the Union Army. Who would want to be the last to die in a defeat?

The 30th may have fired the last shots of the Army of Northern Virginia. Early in the morning of 9 April, Cox's brigade was ordered to fall back but was not given news of the cease-fire that was actually in place. As they retreated, a few men of the 30th fired on advancing federal cavalry who, knowing of the cease-fire, did not return fire. That afternoon the remnants of the 30th North Carolina surrendered and were paroled. The 30th saw 1,506 men serve from 1861 to 1865. One hundred fifty-three surrendered or were paroled at Appomattox Court House.

Global Casualities

*"...familiarity with battle-fields has hardened my feel-
ings very much. Dead men are only less common than
live ones."*
— William Sillers, 22 March 1863

Five hundred and sixty-one of the 1,506 men who served with the 30th died. It is a staggering number and even more shocking as percentage—37.25 percent dead.[17] It is well known that in the Civil War, as in all modern wars prior to the twentieth century, more men died of disease than of combat injury. The 30th was no exception.

The first man to die was Raymond G. Sellers (Company C) on 18 August 1861. He had enlisted in Brunswick County at the age of 18 on 18 July 1861. One month later he was dead of "fever." The last man to die was Private William H. Jones[18] (Company D) of Wake County who had enlisted 1 April 1864. He was captured in Amelia County, Virginia, on 6 April 1865 and died in confinement on 23 June 1865 of "chronic dysentery."

The global numbers are as follows: 128 (8.5 percent) killed or missing in action; 87 (5.87 percent) died of wounds received and 347 (23 percent) died from causes other than combat.[19] One man was killed trying to escape capture as a deserter, and one man accidently drowned.[20] There is some uncertainty in the numbers in that 72 of the 346 died from "unknown" causes according to the records. It is very unlikely that these men were killed in battle and far more likely they died of disease, and they are included in that total. In sum, 215 (14.3 percent) died from combat and 347 (23 percent) from disease.[21]

Two hundred and sixty-six men, or 17.72 percent of the total, were wounded. However, when you examine wounds over time the numbers are starker. Of the 266 men, 121 were wounded two times; 32 were wounded three times; and four men suffered four separate wounds. Therefore, if you consider wounds over time or by battle rather than by individuals, the number of wounded casualties jumps to 464 which would be 30.91 percent.[22]

The Confederate Army did have ambulances and made efforts to get the wounded away from battlefields and into hospitals, but even when successful the process was wholly unsatisfactory. Most transportation was not up to the level of an ambulance. B.C. Jackson was wounded in the knee at Gettysburg and was sent back to Virginia along with other wounded ahead of the regiment. He described his trip this way, "I had a time a coming home. I traveled twelve dase in the rudest waging [wagoning] you ever saw. They got me to Stanton in the 12 days.... I got aboard of the train the next morning. They freight me here in 11 hours."[23]

Many wounds that should not have been fatal were so given the state of medical knowledge and treatment. Sergeant J.B. Ellen[24] (Company D) was wounded and captured at Kelly's Ford. He was struck by a ball which entered four inches to the right of the "spinous processes, between the tenth and eleventh ribs, and merged between the eighth and ninth ribs, in a line with the middle of the axilla. The eighth and ninth ribs were fractured near the wound of exit. The track of the ball was five inches long."[25] The surgeons considered the wound to be non-penetrating despite coughing, labored breathing and blood-tinged expectorate. Sergeant Ellen was treated with "diuretics, expectorants, with sedative to procure sleep, tonics and nutrients, with stimulants, and iodine locally, in form of tincture, over the chest, as a counter-irritant." On 8 December, Ellen awoke from a dream at 4:30 a.m., coughing violently and with much effusion in the right chest. Surgeons introduced a trocar into the right chest which produced the exit of 38 fluid ounces of pus. Stimulants were freely administered. At 7:30 a.m. on 9 December he said he felt strong but at 9:45 a.m. he died. The necropsy showed right lung collapsed and congestion on left but no sign of pneumonia.

Some wounded were simply furloughed home to recover if the wound was not life-threatening. This was often done simply to make room in the hospital. One surgeon offered a harsh criticism of the practice as concerning Sergeant James N. Fuller[26] (Company G). Fuller was wounded at Charlestown, West Virginia, 21 August 1864 by a "ball which passed through his leg making a partial fracture of the fibula. Rather than treatment he was furloughed for sixty days from Staunton General Hospital and suffered a contraction of gastrocnemius which rendered him unable to rest his heel on the ground."[27]

Many men commented on the shock of seeing piles of legs and arms outside field hospitals after battle. Large numbers of wounds to arms and legs, especially when bones were badly shattered or if there was fear of gangrene, resulted in amputation. It is probably impossible to know how many of the 30th North Carolina suffered amputation. The *Medical and Surgical History of the War of the Rebellion* (MSHWR)[28] contains information on the following: eight amputations of arms with one death; six amputations of one leg below the knee; eight amputations from the thigh with three deaths; and one man with both great toes amputated. There were surely more.

Some wounds were truly horrifying to fellow soldiers and even to surgeons. We will confine ourselves here to two examples. First, a man only described as Private Henry C. B_____, Company F, 30th North Carolina, had his entire lower jaw shot away within one and one-half inch of the angles at the Battle of Antietam in September 1862. He was captured and admitted to Hospital No. 5, Frederick, Maryland, and did not die until 17 December 1862. Death described as resulting from "exhaustion and inanition."[29]

Private Charles Center (Company H), received a gunshot wound of the face in the Battle of the Wilderness, 7 May 1864.

> The missile entered the left temple, passing obliquely anteriorly, and emerging one inch below the left eye, severely fracturing and comminuting the superior maxilla, and completely destroying the nasal bones. He was among the captured wounded sent on hospital transports to Washington, and on May 14th was admitted to Carver Hospital. He was very low, and in a comatose state, requiring considerable exertion to arouse him sufficiently to partake of food and stimulants, which were freely administered. He took a quart of milk punch daily. Detergent lotions were applied to the wound. The contents of the left orbit were evacuated, and the vision was destroyed in the right eye. Inflammation gradually extended to the brain; but without any very violent symptoms. The patient survived twenty days, death resulting May 27th, 1864.[30]

After an autopsy was done of Private Center, the surgeons sent a detailed description and the skull to the U.S. Army Medical Museum. The case, along with a wood cut of the injury, was included in MSHWR (Figure 10).

Prisoners of War

Four hundred and twenty-seven men were captured by the Union Army; 27 of those were captured more than one time. Therefore, in the broadest numbers 29.11 percent of the 30th would be captured.[31]

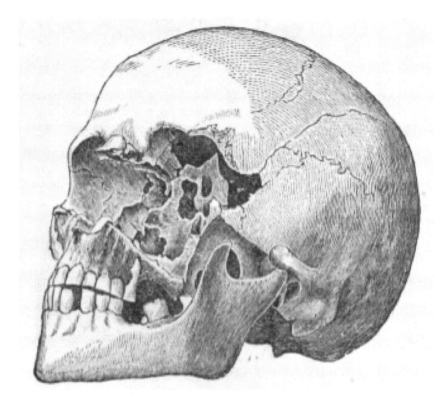

Figure 10. Autopsy Sketch of Charles Center's skull.

In the normal way of measuring casualties, the 30th suffered the following:

Killed or dead of wounds: 211 (14.1 percent)
Died non-combat: 354 (23.65 percent)
Wounded: 266 (17.72 percent)
Captured: 427 (28.44 percent)

This makes a gross total of killed, wounded or captured of 1,258 or 83.91 percent.[32] I made every effort to count each man only once. Otherwise, since many men were wounded, captured and killed, the casualty rate would have been inaccurately over 100 percent.

A different way of viewing casualties is to consider how many of the 30th survived the war neither wounded nor captured. This number was very small. The records show 92 men, just 6 percent, were so fortunate. Two of those transferred out of the 30th in early April

1865 and 16 were not with the unit at Appomattox. They could have been away with or without permission, but all were paroled in other places after the surrender indicating that they had gone AWOL. One thousand, five hundred and six men served in the 30th, and only 6.72 percent of them survived the war without capture or being wounded. Twenty-two of these survivors enlisted in the spring of 1862, 13 in 1863 and 11 in 1864. Enlistment dates are unknown for the final nine but it is unlikely that they joined in 1861. The most fortunate of all men in the regiment were the 37 who enlisted in 1861 (4 percent of 1861 enlistments) who were never wounded or captured, survived disease and privation and surrendered in April 1865.

Here is the final tally of the fates of the 1,506 men and officers of the 30th at the end of the war: 215 (14.3 percent) were killed or died of wounds; 349 (23 percent) died from non-combat reasons; 280 (18.6 percent) were discharged or detailed away from the regiment; 45 (2.9 percent) were absent wounded; 117 (7.8 percent) were prisoners of war; 300 (20 percent) were deserters or AWOL; 36 (2.4 percent) were not with the unit, probably not yet listed as deserters; and 153 (10.5 percent) surrendered at Appomattox (Figure 11).

Non-combat Deaths	23%
Deserted	20%
Discharged or Detailed from Regiment	18.6%
Killed or Dead of Wounds	14.3%
Surrendered at Appomattox	10.5%
Prisoners of War	7.8%
Absent Wounded	2.9%
Unaccounted for, Probably Deserted	2.4%

Figure 11. Strength at Appomattox

8

Survival and Death in the Regiment

Men seldom go to war expecting to die. They understand that war and death are linked, but none expects for death to find him. Each looks to be among the victorious survivors. In 19th- and 20th-century wars a great many died, and if a soldier is on the losing side or has a short supply of that most important asset in war—luck—he is unlikely to survive.

In the Civil War, men of both armies faced terrible odds against survival. The odds were even worse for Confederates because of lack of food, medicine and clothing. In this chapter we will discuss more precise details on survival and death. How likely was a man to die? What factors, other than luck, strongly affected a man's chances of survival?

During its active duty, the 30th suffered 90 percent attrition—1,506 men and officers were enrolled and only 153 surrendered on 9 April 1865. Obviously not all of the 90 percent died or were captured, though many did suffer those fates. Over the course of three years, increasing numbers of men deserted, or went AWOL. Some transferred to other units; some never returned from furloughs. Many finished the war in a hospital. Some were dismissed from the service on grounds of being unfit for duty because of wounds or disease.

The Problem

The lack of record-keeping and reporting by both armies in the Civil War is stunning to the modern mind. The United States Army on its official website estimates that only 60 percent of Union soldiers who died in battle or in a hospital were correctly identified.[1] The Confederate Army was probably even more deficient in identifying its dead. Begin with the fact that company and regimental records were kept haphazardly and that soldiers had no proper identification on them corresponding to dog tags. Neither army had any unit comparable to modern Graves Registration. No units, or persons, were charged with identifying or burying bodies. Surviving company musters and pay rolls—many Confederate records were destroyed—very often listed men as missing, AWOL, or absent for months after they had been killed or taken prisoner. In the first year of the war, before the 30th had seen combat, companies kept lists of men who had died but by late in 1862, as deaths mounted, the effort had been abandoned.[2]

The situation was actually worse for men who died in hospitals from wounds or disease as opposed to battle. No system was in place to report back to units the fate of those individuals. Company records might well list a man as "absent, sent to hospital," sometimes even giving the date on which he left the unit. It was not unusual for such listings to continue for six to ten months after a man had died or deserted from the hospital.[3]

Finally, there were no procedures for informing families that their sons or brothers were dead. When men wrote home they often remarked on who was wounded or dead, but this was unofficial. Local newspapers made occasional efforts to inform the public who had died, but this was sporadic and editors could only interview the survivors to compile lists.[4] It was, therefore, often many months before families and friends learned about deaths. For example, on 30 July 1863 Jacob Gaster of Moore County, North Carolina, addressed a short letter to "Sergeon [*sic*] in charge of the Chimborazo hospital Richmond."[5] He had been told by the captain of Company H that his son, John C. Gaster, had been sent to the hospital toward the end of March. He asks, respectfully, is his son fit, how can he write to him? On the back of the letter it is noted that John Gaster was admitted 1 April, died 9 May and left no effects.

Joseph Hunt wrote to Camp Winder in Richmond on 6 January 1863. He had seen in a Raleigh newspaper that his son James A. Hunt (Company A) was dead. The father asked for information on his son's effects. The letter was answered 10 March 1863.[6]

It was not just men from North Carolina who were not reported by hospitals. Even men from prominent Virginia families were so treated. In the spring of 1862, the son of General Benjamin W.S. Cabell died at Chimborazo Hospital in Richmond. No one in his family even knew he was there. The general berated the Chimborazo director James Brown McCaw on the point and asked why all, whether humble or enabled, were not informed of relations admitted. McCaw responded on 5 April that the hospital had admitted 2,900 men in March and it was simply impossible to inform that many families.[7]

Illness was so pervasive and frequently so debilitating that it will not be surprising that faking sickness was one way to escape duty and danger. In December 1862, Private Robert Wolfe requested pay for time he had been in the hospital but had the bad luck that his claim was investigated. His company commander wrote that Wolfe had been AWOL since 17 September 1862. "He pretends to have rheumatism. Last summer he imposed on our surgeon and the company until they were reduced to the necessity of forcing him on duty ... found nothing the matter. He has been reported a deserter."[8]

Another result of the lack of any reporting by hospitals is that they were not only used as places to attempt to escape duty and danger but to facilitate desertion. "Deserted from hospital" is a fairly common entry in hospital records on individuals. Wounded or partially disabled men were often assigned duty as hospital guards. One must assume that these guards were intended more to prevent desertion than to protect patients. Hartwell Butler (Company A) was released from the hospital in June 1863. He took the opportunity to vanish and never returned to his company.[9]

During the four years from April 1861 through April 1865, 1,506 men served in the 30th North Carolina.[10] Their length of service would vary from one day—two men who deserted the same day they joined—to over 1,500 days—seven men who were prisoners of war not released until June 1865. In the broadest sense, 942 men (62.43 percent) survived or at least were alive when they left the regiment or when the war ended. However, 242 men out of the 942 survivors left the regiment because they were no longer fit for service. They had become so crippled or were so debilitated from wounds, disease or service conditions that they were discharged, assigned to the Invalid Corps (mostly amputees) or more or less permanently hospitalized or furloughed. There is no way to know how many of these discharged men were able to lead productive lives after returning home. If we add those who were crippled in some way to the dead, then 809 men (53.61 percent) died or were crippled by the war.

Seven hundred men were fortunate enough to survive the war or leave the regiment, presumably in decent health. When the regiment surrendered at Appomattox Court House, 256 men were away from the regiment for various reasons—detailed elsewhere, on furlough, or they had simply left the unit but were not yet listed as deserters; 97 had resigned (when the regiment was reorganized in May 1862 many officers who were not reelected resigned and went home) or had transferred to other units; 16 had provided a substitute; 53 were officially listed as deserted or AWOL; 120 were prisoners of war. There are two important points to note on the prisoners of war. First, late in 1864 into early 1865 the Union paroled many prisoners back to the Confederacy. Only a few of these men went back into the ranks. Most were considered by surgeons as too debilitated to serve and were either hospitalized or sent home on extended furlough. Some of the freed prisoners deserted rather than return to the war. At the same time that the Union was paroling or exchanging prisoners, the number of men deserting to the Union Army began to rise. Surrender/desertion removed men from combat but often did not serve them well. Sanitary conditions in many of the prisons, especially Elmira, New York, were atrocious, and 70 men of the 30th North Carolina died of disease in Union prisons.[11] Eighteen who were captured wounded died as well, but all indications are that the wounded were given hospital care on the same level as Union wounded.

The Numbers

The information will be presented in three ways. First, what factors seem to have improved or worsened chances at survival? Second, how many men died of what cause over the course of time and, third, how much more likely was a man to die of disease rather than combat? We will give a detailed analysis on death by disease in the following chapter.

There are many criteria that might have correlated with increased or decreased survivability—rank; age; social status; farm or non-farm origin; the company to which a man belonged; volunteer, conscript or substitute status; and length of service and exposure to death.

Social status as a simple criterion seems to have had little correlation to death. We classified men into four groups based on occupation and census reports: Laborers (farm and non-farm); Small Farmers and Craftsmen; Middling Farmers and Merchants; Wealthy Farmers and Professionals. Only Middling Farmers showed any significant variation from the others. Regression analysis showed they were only 42 percent as likely to survive as other social categories (Figure 12).

	Coefficients	Standard Error	Wald Test	Degrees of Freedom	t-Value	Prob>t	Odds Ratio
Age at Enlistment	-0.03469059	0.009541808 0.009542	13.21788714	1	-3.635641228	2.77E-04	0.965904231
Conscript	-0.644217362	0.217354244	8.78473371	1	-2.963905145	0.003037619	0.525073323
Officers	-0.851337116	0.307669317	7.656578895	1	-2.767052384	0.005656567	0.42684381
Middling Farmers	-0.870308161	0.391712694	4.936405413	1	-1.221802289	0.02629667	0.418822465

Figure 12. Regression Analysis of Four Factors

Volunteers, Conscripts and Substitutes

A volunteer had only a 53 percent chance of survival as opposed to a conscript. The most likely reason for this has to do with when and how conscription was carried out. The first draft was held in the spring of 1862. By that point roughly 1,000 volunteers had already joined the regiment, and 50 of them were already dead of disease. The lateness of the draft also meant that most of those conscripted missed the killing fields of Gaines Mill, Malvern Hill and Antietam. Arriving late was a great advantage.

Second, many if not most of the conscripts were reluctant to become soldiers. Some were openly opposed to the war and were forced in at gunpoint. They were, therefore, more prone than volunteers to desert, to fake illness or to find ways to avoid combat and when possible escape all together. Volunteers who had been in the regiment since 1861 had developed much stronger loyalty to the regiment and to their comrades which tended to lessen desertion.

Two tests returned only null significance. There was no difference in survival between farmers and non-farmers. Nor did the company to which a man belonged affect survival. The companies were raised at different times at different places; therefore, there could have been some influence. There was not.

Rank was an important determinant of survival (Figure 13). Logistic regression showed that an enlisted man had only 42.7 percent chance to survive compared to an officer. The level of officer rank was also very important. The old adage that the higher the rank the less

Rank	Total	Dead	%	Crippled	%	%D or C
Private	1205	489	40.581%	208	17.26%	57.842%
Musician	17	2	11.765%	4	23.53%	35.294%
Corporal	83	21	25.301%	10	12.05%	37.349%
Sergeant	78	31	39.744%	4	5.13%	44.872%
1st Sergeant	19	5	26.316%	0	0.00%	26.316%
Sgt. Major	9	0	0.000%	3	33.33%	33.333%
3rd Lt	16	4	25.000%	3	18.75%	43.750%
2nd Lt	20	5	25.000%	1	5.00%	30.000%
1st Lt	22	4	18.182%	3	13.64%	31.818%
Captain	26	5	19.231%	3	11.54%	30.769%
Major	10	0	0.000%	1	10.00%	10.000%
Lt. Col	3	1	33.333%	1	33.33%	66.667%
Colonel	1	0	0.000%		0.00%	0.000%
TOTALS	1509	567	37.575%	242	16.04%	53.612%

Figure 13. Survival by Rank

likely the death proved correct with the exception of sergeants who died at very near the same rate as privates. The only ranks that were nearly immune to death were the non-combat ranks of major, administrative sergeants such as commissary sergeant or sergeant major and musicians. The variation among lieutenants is explained by the fact that many 1st lieutenants were either executive officers or company commanders in the absence of captains.

While considering rank, let us take advantage of one opportunity to show the presence of luck. The commander of the regiment, Colonel Francis Parker, came within a millimeter of death twice. Once, he was wounded in the face and very nearly drowned in his own blood and was presumed for a while to be dead. A second time, a bullet creased his skull taking out a furrow of bone and exposing the membrane covering his brain. After that wound he placed a sponge over the furrow under his hat to prevent injury to his brain. Despite his wounds, which convinced Confederate authorities to permit him to leave the army in 1864, his life after the war seems not to have been impaired.

Age at Joining

War is fought by young men for obvious reasons. Age as a determinant of survival turned out to be of overwhelming importance. The logistic regression showed that for each year older than the age of 18 a man was when he enrolled—all other things being equal—he was 3.4 percent less likely to survive.

Disease or Combat

The greatest hazard facing men in the Civil War was disease rather than battle.[12] For a man involved in pitched battle, survival—assuming he did not flee or find some way to avoid advancing—seems to have been largely a question of luck. Luck is not knowable or quantifiable; therefore, we do not treat it. For the sake of this story we presume luck, like bravery or fear, was evenly distributed throughout the regiment.

Disease on the other hand was not so unbiased. Did a man have any immunity to pathogens when he joined? Was he of a robust constitution or was he weak? It is clear that the general health of men volunteering in 1861 was not good. Physicians rejected many in the fall of 1861 as unfit for service. Of those approved by physicians, 50 proved unable to stand the rigors of training and were discharged before the regiment first faced combat in the Seven Days Campaign. Fifty additional men had died of disease.

The raw numbers make it clear, as expected, that a man was more likely to die of disease than of battle—349 died of disease and 215 in battle. What we wanted to know was how consistent was that likelihood and how strong was it. We, therefore, subjected the data to a Kaplan-Meier analysis (Figure 14). This test is designed to compare survivability of two cohorts. We compared the likelihood of a man

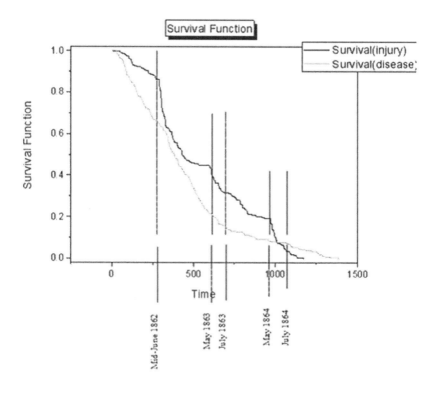

Figure 14. Kaplan-Meier Test on Survivability

dying from disease or combat from the date of the first death (September 1861) to the last death (June 1865).

Both lines on this chart are interesting. The dark line showing probability of death by battle pulsates, as one would expect, dropping steeply in major battles and sloping more gently through small skirmishes or where the regiment was not engaged in combat.

The pale line showing probability of death by disease on the other hand, slopes at a very consistent angle from September 1861 through the summer of 1863 when the angle decreases to a new consistency which it maintains until the last death in a POW camp in June 1865.

The most striking conclusion from the Kaplan-Meier analysis is that at each point until the summer of 1864, a man was more likely to die of disease than of battle. Only from July to October 1864 was a man more likely to die of battle. From October 1864 through the spring of 1865, there were no battle deaths despite the regiment being in the defense of Petersburg and retreating toward Appomattox with the other units of the army. Disease, however, continued to kill at the same rate one month after the surrender.[13]

Length of Service

It would be reasonable to assume that the longer a man was exposed to disease and battle the more likely he would be to die—reasonable but not valid. The opposite would seem to be true. We examined how many men died or were crippled by length of service in blocks of 100 days. Overall, 567 men (37.58 percent of the regiment) died and 242 (16.04 percent) were crippled. Combined, this meant 53.61 percent of the regiment. Regardless of when a man enrolled, he seems to have had nearly the same chance of dying or being crippled. The only exception was those who joined in the third quarter of 1861 and those who joined in 1864. The number who joined in 1864 was too small to have statistical validity. Those from the second quarter of 1861 included many men who resigned or left the unit before the summer of 1862 thereby escaping both disease and combat.

The clear conclusion is that a man was far more likely to die soon after joining the regiment. If he survived through one season of combat, his chances of continued survival rose dramatically. No doubt this was due to increased understanding of battle and some acquired immunity to disease. It is also consistent with stories from other wars that hardened veterans tended to live and new recruits died.

Figure 15 shows how many died by length of service. For example, in the third quarter of 1861, 817 enrolled in the regiment and 174 of them died. Nineteen, 10.92 percent of the 174 dead, died before they had served 100 days.

There are several striking conclusions to be drawn about survivability in the Civil War. The first is the stunning advantage of youth. Statistically, for every year over 18 a man was when joining, he was 3.4 percent less likely to survive. A man of 40 years was, therefore, 75 percent less likely to live than one aged 18. Second, the advantage of rank is clear. This is not surprising and probably true of all wars. Third, the consistent greater danger of disease rather than combat death is clearly shown by the Kaplan-Meier analysis. Disease was always the greater killer even in times of combat. Finally, the advantage of staying alive through the first campaign increased a man's likelihood of surviving the war by a great deal.

Days served When joined	<100	100-200	200-300	300-400	400-500	500-600	600-700	700-800	800-900	900-1K	1K-1100	1100-1200	1200-1300	1300-1400	No dead	No enrolled
3Q61	19	12	9	33	27	30	9	3	7	2	4	6	9	4	174	817
	10.92%	6.9%	5.17%	18.97%	15.52	17.24	5.17	1.72	4.02	1.15	2.3	3.45	5.17	2.3		
1Q62	4	3	5	10	5	1	3	1	1	1	3	1			38	150
	10.53%	7.89%	13.16%	26.32%	13.16	2.63	7.89	2.63	2.63	2.63	7.89	2.63				
2Q62	2	6	6	3	0	3	1	1	2	1	1				26	105
	7.69%	23.08%	23.08%	11.54%	0	11.54	3.85	3.85	7.69	3.85	3.85					
3Q62	8	11	2	3	3	2	1	1	2						33	81
	24.24%	33.33%	6.06%	9.09%	9.09	6.06	3.03	3.03	6.06							
3Q63	4	9	7	4	7	5	2								38	141
	10.53	23.68%	18.42%	10.53%	18.42	13.16	5.26									
64	2	2	1	2	1										8	38
	25%	25%	12.5%	25%	12.5											
Total	39	43	30	55	43	41	16	6	12	4	8	7	9	4	317	1332
	12.3%	13.56%	9.46%	17.35%	13.56	12.93	5.05	1.89	3.79	1.26	2.52	2.21	2.84	1.26		

Figure 15. Deaths by Number of Days of Service

9

Death by Disease

*"I think I must to of seen a thousand [sick men] in the
three Hospittles. It has nearly put me out of the notion
of volunteering."*
—Abel Douglass to Louis McLeod, 13 April 1862

Disease was the great enemy of both armies in the Civil War. Even
before the 30th North Carolina assembled near Wilmington, one man
had died of "fever" in mid–August.[1] On the very days that the men
were gathering at Camp Wyatt, 29 and 30 September 1861, two more
died of afflictions that would destroy so many men—pneumonia and
typhoid fever. By the time the 30th suffered its first battle causality at
Gaines Mill on 27 June 1862, 56 men had been discharged for health
reasons and 47 were dead of disease: three of "fever"; 18 of typhoid;
six of pneumonia; two of "brain fever" (probably meningitis); three
of acute diarrhea; one of measles; one of phthisis; one of erysipelas;
one of consumption; one of mumps; one of "bilious fever," which could
have been any one of several diseases including typhoid fever; nine of
"disease" or unspecified causes.

General State of Health

The 1860s were the last years in the Western world that produced
such terrible rates of sickness and death. Everything was bad, from the
general health of the men to poor medical knowledge of physicians
and surgeons. Hospitals were little better than incubation pools for
disease.

The state of health of many volunteers in 1861 was abysmal. For the first six months, the regiment apparently had no official surgeons and physicians informally spent what time they could with the men to treat disease.[2] As the 30th was forming, these physicians rejected dozens of men as being unfit.[3] Many of those who passed the muster were healthy only by comparison to those rejected. They were of a feeble constitution and unable to bear the strain of training. In addition to the 56 men (roughly 5 percent) discharged for debility, sickness or other weakness, one man was sent home under-aged; one over-aged, and one for larceny.[4] When combined with men dead of disease during the same period, it means the regiment had lost nearly 10 percent of its strength for reasons of health before its first battle at Gaines Mill.[5]

EXAMPLE: James Ross[6] was drafted and joined the regiment in March 1862 and was hospitalized four times before the year was over: May in Wilmington for cholera; September at General Hospital #24 in Richmond for chronic kidney infection; October, to the same hospital for spinal pain and in December to Chimborazo for dropsy. On 30 June 1863, he was discharged for health reasons.

Even men relatively healthy and fit were often rendered unable to train due to various diseases. The great majority of soldiers had lived a relatively isolated rural life. They had rarely been exposed to infectious disease. Therefore, when they were brought together in large numbers in army camps, it is hardly surprising that epidemics tore through the regiment. For the remaining three years of service, the men would continue to be struck with disease in addition to battlefield trauma. The treatment they received was at best palliative and often actually harmful. Accurate diagnoses of conditions were not the norm, and the education of physicians, much less assistant surgeons, was often grossly inadequate.

By the end of the war, 349 (23 percent of total enrollment) would be dead of disease and 125 (8 percent) discharged for health reasons. We know the precise disease for 265 of the dead. Four conditions accounted for over 75 percent of deaths: typhoid 30 percent; pneumonia 20 percent; dysentery or diarrhea 17 percent[7] and small pox 10 percent (Figure 16).

The largest number of disease-related deaths occurred during winter months. Men were in close contact with each other in either tents or sheds, with poor sanitation. The only exception to this pattern is the summer spike in typhoid, contracted from contaminated water (Figure 17).

"Our entire Regiment has the diarrhea."
—John G. Witherspoon,
16 July 1862

Impact of Disease

Disease not only killed large numbers, but perhaps even more crucial, it incapacitated many others who were hospitalized, furloughed home or confined

KNOWN CONDITION	NO OF DEATHS
Brain Fever	7
Erysipelas	3
Phthisis	3
Scurvy	3
Consumption	2
Died Suddenly	2
Gangrene	2
Pyaemia	2
Abscessed lung	1
Acute Bronchitis	1
Anasarca	1
Bowel Consumption	1
Camp Fever (Typhus)	1
Congestion of Lungs	1
Congestion of brain	1
Congestive Chill	1
Dropsy	1
Exhaustion	1
Malaria	1
Acute Gastritis	1
Hemorrhage of bowels	1
Hernia	1
Measles	1
Mumps	1
Pleurisy	1
Rheumatism	1
Scarlet Fever	1
Tonsillitis	1

Figure 16. Other Causes of Death

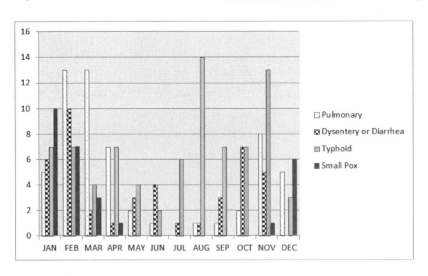

Figure 17. Death from Disease by Month

96

to quarters, thereby preventing training or causing men to drop out before battles. The surviving regimental rosters and reports from early in the war give only a rough idea of how many were sick. Rosters have survived for most companies dated around 10 October, 31 October and 31 December 1861. If a man was hospitalized or furloughed it might have been noted but without much detail. Even so, the number of men so reported in late 1861 was staggering. In October, 159 men were reported hospitalized, sick or unfit for duty. Given that the regiment numbered only about 800 in October, this represents 20 percent of its strength. Reports from November and December showed 55 men who fell ill during those months. The reports did not indicate those who had not yet returned from earlier sickness. On 17 November 1861, John G. Witherspoon wrote his wife that more than half the regiment was "not fit for duty."[8]

Letters written home were filled with accounts of who was sick, who was in the hospital, who was unable to drill and, too often, who had died. In September and October 1861, the number of officers and men on the roster of Company H was 94. In May 1862, the number had grown to 120. However, the number of men available for duty was always far below those numbers. The letters of Louis McLeod are especially revealing in this regard. Nearly every letter talked about how many men were sick and what diseases were sweeping through the company and regiment. It is illustrative to look at some of McLeod's comments.

2 October 1861. The 30th had just arrived near Wilmington, and they shared a field with a second regiment: 2,000 men in close contact with inadequate sanitation facilities. There were large numbers of measles and "hooping cough. The cough is the worst I ever saw. I was on gard last knight and I never herd as much coughing in my life. I never slep any at all."

5 October 1861. "There is forty or fifty [close to half of the company] in the horspittle at this time [very bad off with colds]." They were perhaps suffering from influenza, meningitis or any of several "fevers" ripping through the camp. Certainly they did not just have colds.

30 October 1861. McLeod reports he, and others, are just about over the cold "only my neck is a little sore yet." The length of sickness coupled with sore neck would suggest meningitis. Most of the company had recovered from the measles except eight or ten. Some others had some kind of fever, and two were so sick that the captain sent them home along with a third man to look after them.

17 November 1861. McLeod himself caught the big measles.[9] He had been in bed for three days, and the doctor said he would not be fit for duty for three weeks. His tent mate and dear friend Francis Moore was down with "Belious Feaver" and gone home.

2 December 1861. Twenty members of Company H were too sick to drill at all. "Good many cases of mumps." Some were just back drilling after recovering from the mumps. At least 12 men who had been home sick just returned.

4 April 1862. No mention of disease but the camp had been moved and because no wells had been dug they were getting their water from creeks. On 13 April 1862, McLeod was very sick for several days with a slight touch of the "Billious feavar," almost certainly typhoid from drinking creek water. He hoped to be able to drill again the next day. Company mostly had colds and coughs though some had measles.

20 April 1862. McLeod had drilled on Monday, 14 April and since then was back in bed with the fever. The captain had gone home at the same time with bilious fever. Three companies, including Company H, had been ordered to Jacksonville but 13 men, including McLeod, were too sick to march. Some of them had measles.

28 April 1862. McLeod recovered but lost 10 pounds and was now back with the company. Quite a few men had measles, including his wife's cousin. Five members of the company had to be left in Wilmington.

10 June 1862. McLeod had not been able to drill for three days because of bad "bowel complaint." Half the company was unable to perform duty due to dysentery but only two men were in the hospital. John Witherspoon noted "a great many sick in the Regt. At this time" on 5 June.

15 June 1862. McLeod and many others have had such dysentery that they could not drill or even travel. The regiment left for Virginia, but he and 21 other members of the company were left behind. There were also others (number not given) in the hospital.

22 June 1862. McLeod and six members of the company traveled to Richmond to rejoin the company. McLeod secured furloughs for all the others that were too sick to travel and sent them home. It is doubtful that McLeod and the other six men were very healthy. They were simply able to travel.

What is even more striking about McLeod's comments is that few of the men he refers to as unable to train so appear in the company records. The official records indicate 750 men present for most of the period from November 1861 through May 1862. From letters it is clear that very often there must have been 35 to 40 percent of the regiment unfit for duty and on occasion probably in excess of 50 percent. As the men gained immunity to some diseases, the percentage of those out sick would decline going forward, but the amount of sickness would remain high throughout the war.

Medical Care

> *"I had a mustard plaster on my bowels that nearly raised a blister which has annoyed me a good deal as it had been quite sore."*
> —John Witherspoon, 5 June 1862

Begin with the simple fact that all physicians and surgeons were groping in the dark with no real understanding of pathogens and actual causes of diseases.[10] While some physicians, like Lister and Oliver Wendell Holmes, were beginning to urge hand-washing and use of sterilizing procedures, most saw no point at all in those time-consuming efforts. As the famous Philadelphia physician Charles Delulcena Meigs put it in the 1850s: "A physician is a gentleman, and a gentleman's hands are always clean."[11]

During the Civil War, there was only rudimentary understanding of how disease spread or of its causes.[12] Sanitation in army camps was limited, hardly any more advanced than what Roman legions had practiced. When thousands of men who had lived fairly isolated lives were brought together in close quarters with poor sanitation, the result was inevitable.

Vaccination was available only for small pox, and its use was far from universal. Tragically, in 1862 when the Confederate Army vaccinated large numbers of men, the serum was contaminated and not only proved ineffective against small pox but sickened many and even killed some. B.C. Jackson spent the fall of 1862 in Chimborazo and Winder Hospitals for extreme back and leg pain. While there he was vaccinated for small pox. However, he reported that he was vaccinated five times "before it taken."[13] There were no governmental provisions for civilian vaccination. Many at home were forced to rely on self-vaccination when they could do so. John Witherspoon sent his wife two scabs for that purpose in the winter of 1862. One fresh one he took from a member of another company and one off his own arm which represented the third attempt at his own vaccination.[14] B.C. Jackson asked his brother to see if the local physician wanted his scab; if so, he would send it.[15]

Since causation was very poorly understood, diagnoses were often based on symptoms common to many diseases. Sometimes different symptoms of one disease might be considered to be separate diseases. The fact that most physicians still wrote their diagnoses in Latin—often bastardized Latin used by men who did not truly know the language—confused things even more.

Medical records of hospitalization, furloughs and deaths for the 30th North Carolina contain more than a gross of terms, some in Latin, some in English, some only descriptions of symptoms and some fairly precise identification of maladies. To take the terms literally would be to build confusion on top of poor understanding. What is essential is to interpret the records in modern terms whenever possible.

Diagnoses and Treatment of Disease

> *"[H]e was nearly well though there remained some dropsical swelling of foot and leg for which a mixture of squill, buchu and sweet spirit of nitre was administered."*
> —Treatment for scurvy given to
> Private Alexander Robinson

In the decade after the war, the U.S. Surgeon General's office made an encyclopedic effort to analyze the medical history of both Union and Confederate soldiers, hoping that surgical techniques and medicine would be improved by learning from the war experience.[16] This massive work summarized the state of medical knowledge at the time, interpreted Civil War records in the light of somewhat improved medical knowledge after the war and gave thousands of case studies of surgical and medical treatments. The editors also abandoned all Latin in favor of clear English terms. It is the essential source for understanding Civil War medicine. We will begin by drawing on the surgeon general's report for a brief discussion of how several major diseases were understood and reported during the war.

The most confusion may have been in diagnosing "fevers" as diseases rather than a symptom of a disease. Given that a great many diseases produce fevers in the human body, confusion was inevitable. Most pre–Civil War medical authorities described three large categories of fevers: eruptive, continuing and intermittent.

Eruptive fevers included mostly diseases that were fairly easy to identify due to patterns of skin eruption like small pox, chicken pox (not yet seen as a separate disease from small pox) and measles.

Continuing fever was already an obsolete term in 1860 but it was still used by physicians who could not, or would not, distinguish between typhoid and typhus.[17] By 1860, most physicians could identify the symptoms of typhoid fever. Therefore, typhoid—called both typhoid and typhoid pneumonia—is a frequent entry in the records.

> *"I have had the rumatic pains very badley indeed &*
> *I feel stiff in my joints yet but the pains has abated*
> *considerable."*
> —A.A. Jackson, 26 March 1863

Intermittent fevers seem to have been various ways of describing malaria. "Remittent fever," "intermittent fever," "congestive intermittent fever," and "quotidian remittent fever" were all descriptions of the most common form of malaria in which the chills and fevers last for one day and can return in one day. "Tertian remittent fever" is a less common form of the disease in which chills and fevers return in two days. The least common of all is quartan, or quartones, remittent fever in which chills and fevers return in three days.[18] Due to the various possible symptoms of malaria, which include in addition to fevers and shivering, headache, joint pain, vomiting, jaundice, retinal damage and convulsions, many "diseases" that are listed—ague, jaundice, nyctalopia, hemeralopia, epilepsy and especially acute rheumatism could have been due to malaria.[19] The editors of the *MSHWR* insisted that the number of cases of malaria was considerably under-reported in the Union Army. They believed that many cases of general dropsy, abdominal dropsy and dropsy from hepatic disease were actually malaria.[20] They included very little information on malaria in the Confederate Army, but there is no reason to think that reporting in that army was any better. Therefore, numbers given for malaria in the 30th North Carolina are almost certainly too low.

Some of the diagnoses given during the war are especially unhelpful: *rheumatismas acutus; catarrhus* (*catarrhus epidem* was certainly influenza); *rheum acuta*. These terms have obvious English equivalents, but they are not satisfactory medical terms. Both *rheum* and *catarrhus* indicate copious discharge of mucus and would usually be considered as colds or some influenza-like affliction. The men themselves in letters referred to very bad colds that lasted for weeks and which left lingering symptoms. True colds only last 14 days or less. It is hardly reasonable that the 17 men hospitalized for *rheum acuta* (two so ill that they were furloughed to recover) and the 45 hospitalized for *catarrhus* were suffering simple colds. It is also practically impossible that 59 men hospitalized for *rheumatismas acutus* (six having to be furloughed to recover) truly suffered from rheumatism. The most likely reality for *rheumatismas* was complications from malaria. There are so many possibilities for *rheum* and *catarrhus* that we will include them as categories under infectious diseases rather than arbitrarily assigning them to typhoid, influenza or some other fever. The medical history of individual soldiers can offer some clarification. For example, Louis Hornaday[21] contracted malaria (*febris remittens*) in June 1862. In September, he was admitted to the Danville hospital for acute rheumatism. In one case, it is possible to see what a patient's real problem was. W.H. Brown (Company F) was admitted to Farmville Hospital on 11 June 1863 with "*rheum acuta*." However, his real problem seems to have been "subacute inflammation of stomach with enlargement 2 months standing stomach & duodenum."[22]

Another common diagnosis was debility, or *debilitas*, given to 115 men. This was often cited in discharge papers and was routinely given as reason for hospitalization of returning prisoners of war. It is tempting to include these men under malaria. That may well have often been the case. Henry Brinkley (Company K) suffered an attack of "intermittent fever" 20 May 1864, followed by "severe periodical neuralgia." Two months later, 20 July, he was given a 60-day medical furlough for debility.[23] However, some recruits were discharged early as being physically unfit for service, and by the last months of the war it is likely that the health of numerous men simply broke down under the stress of malnutrition and harsh conditions. Therefore, we keep debility as a category.

Finally, over one-quarter of the entries simply say "sick." However, this time it is easier to compensate. The largest concentration of "sick" records, 257 or 44 percent, is in the fall and winter of 1861 when most ill men were sent home or kept in quarters since hospitals were not generally available. We know from letters that the diseases ravaging the regiment—measles, mumps, agues, flu-like conditions and fevers—were precisely those that appear among those admitted to the hospital in Wilmington. The second high count of "sick"—107 cases, 18.3 percent—is September through December 1862. We assume that the "sick" patients suffered the same diseases in the same proportions as the regiment as a whole.

Number of Episodes

According to regimental records, 1,115 of the 1,506 men of the 30th North Carolina died from or suffered at least one episode of sickness or injury severe enough to require hospitalization, furlough or other suspension of duty. Given what we know from individual letters and diaries, it is highly likely that this number is too low and that many illnesses were never reported. We are, therefore, comfortable in asserting our belief that no member of the 30th North Carolina escaped some incidence of serious sickness. For many men, sickness was a frequently recurring brush with death. Of the 1,115 known victims, only 489 appear one time, while 280 men suffered two episodes; 159, three episodes; 80, four episodes; 12 appear five times; six appear six times; 10 appear seven times; and two men show up 10 times in the records. When men who died in combat or as direct result of combat are removed from the data, records show 900 men who suffered

1,997 episodes of sickness, including death from sickness. These are the numbers we will use for percentages and extrapolation to the full complement of 1,506 men.

The clearest way to understand the medical history of the 30th North Carolina is to lump the various diagnoses into several broad categories. The categories we have chosen are: 1. Wounds and injuries, discussed in Chapter 7; 2. Diseases of the skin; 3. Diseases of the heart; 4. Mental disorders; 5. Pulmonary disorders; 6. Afflictions of the throat; 7. Urological and venereal diseases; 8. Bowel disorders; 9. Eruptive fevers; 10. Malaria in its various forms; 11. Typhoid and typhus fever; 12. Other infectious diseases; 13. Non-infectious diseases; and 14. Conditions of unknown cause.

Diseases of the Skin

The most common and the deadliest dermatological disease was erysipelas, a skin infection caused by *streptococcal bacterium*. Ten episodes of erysipelas were recorded between April 1862 and March 1863. Three of the men died, one contracted typhoid in the hospital and died from the second disease and one was given a 30-day furlough home to recover. In the last years of the war, the most common afflictions were scabies—five cases—and ulcers on the body—five cases. One man was hospitalized for *furunulus*. His case must have been exceptional since it is clear from letters that boils were so common as ordinarily not to require hospitalization. Two men suffered from *morbus cutis*, similar to gangrene but of the skin, and two from *paronychia*. All together there were 28 episodes of skin disease (1.4 percent of all episodes), including furloughs for recovery involving 21 men (2.3 percent of all men). Our belief is that these diseases, especially scabies, were probably far more prevalent but only the most severe cases were actually hospitalized.

EXAMPLE: James Griffin[24] was treated for scabies early in November 1863; was given a 30-day sick furlough for the remainder of November 1863; spent late January and early February 1864 hospitalized in Richmond for body ulcers; November 1864 hospitalized for scrofulous ulcers of legs. He was among the large number of men who fled into Union captivity on 3 April 1865.

Diseases of the Heart

All of the incidences of heart diseases seem to have been heart failure or, in 19th-century terms, dropsy. Dropsy referred to buildup of fluid around the heart; seven men were given that diagnosis, one of whom died at home on sick furlough.[25] Four men were diagnosed with *anasarca*, or generalized dropsy. Three of the four were diagnosed in 1862, one dying in December. A third form of generalized dropsy including buildup of fluid in the abdominal cavity, *ascites*, was diagnosed in seven men. Finally, one man's affliction was simply called "heart disease." Admission to hospitals for the various heart diseases were not numerous but tended to be very long—94 days—indicating that these men were very weakened.

Mental Disorders

> "...nostalgia, the home-sickness which wrings the heart and impoverishes the blood, killed many a brave soldier."
> —Phoebe Yates Pember

By modern standards, this smallest category of afflictions is probably the most under-reported. The wars of the 20th and 21st centuries have seen more recognition of the terrible mental toll war extracts from soldiers. Not so in the Civil War. There are no records of "battle fatigue" or "shell shock" or PTSD. Mental problems were assumed to be attempts at escaping combat or simply personality quirks. The four men so diagnosed as suffering from "mania," "acute mania" in one case, and "nostalgia" must have truly been unable to function.

An example of how mental problems were usually dealt with is Labon Dudley of Company H. Sergeant A.F. Harrington thought him "the worst case I ever saw I have seen the time I would be sory for him but I am so hardend that it is as much as I can doo to be sory for myself." The regimental physician refused to excuse Dudley from drill. He said, "[M]ake him drill or stick the bayonet in him."[26]

Pulmonary Disorders

*"We lost one of our best soldiers last night in camp to
pneumonia. He went through every battle with the
company & took sick after the last one."*
—A.A. Jackson, 15 May 1863

We now arrive at a very large group of diagnoses—172 incidences,
8.6 percent of the total, involving 138 men. While several terms are used,
all can be regarded as bronchitis, pleurisy, tuberculosis or pneumonia.
Pleurisy or pleuritis affected seven men, one of whom died. Acute bronchitis was diagnosed in 22 men with one death, and one man suffered
from chronic bronchitis and itch. Tuberculosis, called consumption,
phthisis, scarefula or abscessed lung, was diagnosed in 16 men and killed
five of them. The greatest pulmonary scourge was pneumonia—122
cases plus one chronic pneumonia and one congestion of lungs. Even
when men recovered from wounds they might die from pneumonia as
did Thomas Jackson. The 122 cases resulted in 52 deaths. The average
length of hospitalization for these diseases was 47 days. Pneumonia and
other pulmonary diseases were most likely to occur in late winter when
men were living closely in winter quarters rather than in the field (Figure 18). Louis McLeod had an instinctive understanding of this danger

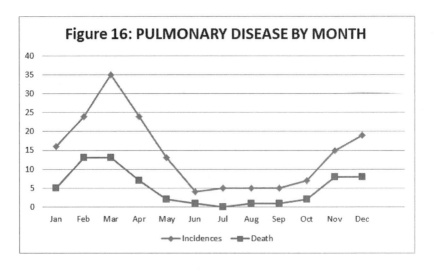

Figure 18. Pulmonary Disease by Month

when he wrote to his wife that winter quarters were almost ready, but he would rather stay in his tent than to go into a house "where there is such a mess and so nasty. I think it will make us all sick."[27]

EXAMPLE: Samuel Graham[28] was admitted in Wilmington for abscesses in March and June of 1862. In August, he died of tuberculous (phthisis).

Afflictions of the Throat

All incidences of this small group occurred in 1862. Four men were described as having laryngitis, one with scrofulous infection of the throat, and four with tonsillitis, one of whom died. It is likely that men suffering from similar disorders later than 1862 were diagnosed in some other way.

Urological and Venereal Diseases

This category covers 29 incidents and 28 men. Nine men were hospitalized with venereal diseases—eight gonorrhea and one syphilis. Kidney disease was diagnosed in three. Bladder inflammation was noted for two men and blockage of urine for three. Five men had inflammation of the testicles while five more suffered from hydrocele or dropsy of the testicles. One man was suffering with corditis.

Diseases of the urinary tract display large differences in days to recover. Gonorrhea sufferers, when they were hospitalized, were released in only six days; the one case of secondary syphilis was held for 22 days—there was of course no cure available. Hospitalizations for bladder and urinary infections or conditions ranged from one to 126 days for an average of 43 days.

Bowel Disorders

> "...had bowel disease but we have that very often. That is not much for a soldier to have."
> —John C. Goodin, 22 May 1863

This category has a large number of cases and was one of the deadliest. One man died of bowel consumption (presumably either tuberculosis or colon cancer), and one man was admitted twice with a fistula of the anus.

The most common bowel condition and one of the terrible killers of the Civil War was what the men referred to as "the bowel complaint"—dysentery or diarrhea. Medical records are filled with entries related to this affliction: acute diarrhea, 113 cases; acute dysentery, 35 cases; chronic, furloughs for convalescing, complications of, and finally death in the case of 47 men, 26 of whom were prisoners of war. These numbers reflect only those cases which were so severe that the patient could not function. The bowel complaint was a constant affliction of many, if not most, men. One who died was Z.R. Roberson (Company G). He was captured 25 September 1864; admitted to a prison hospital 12 October; and treated with alternatives, astringents and tonics. He died 15 December 1864.[29]

EXAMPLE: George Washington Smith[30] spent much of his brief military career sick. In the spring of 1862, he was mostly confined to quarters as unable to perform duty; in May 1862, he was hospitalized in Wilmington with acute diarrhea; in mid–June, he suffered

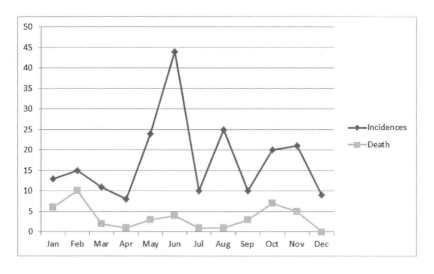

Figure 19. Diarrhea and Dysentery Incidences by Month

malaria (*febris remittens*); on 21 December 1862, he was admitted to Chimborazo with acute diarrhea, dying of that affliction on 16 January 1863.

The average hospital stay for diarrhea and dysentery was 30 days. Many of those terms were cut short by death (Figure 19).

Eruptive Fevers

> *"[S]mall pox I am afraid will almost ruin our army this winter. It seems to be all over the Army and the Confederacy."*
> —John Witherspoon, 3 January 1863

The group of diseases, called collectively eruptive fevers in the 19th century, accounts for 92 episodes involving 75 men. Early in the war, the most common disease was measles or rubeola, with 39 cases including three deaths. Two cases were simply called "eruptive fever." The most common form from 1863–1865, and the most deadly, was small pox. Physicians used several terms for this killer in addition to small pox: *variola, variola confluentia* and *varioloid*. The last could have been a mild case of small pox, a reaction to vaccination or perhaps chicken pox. Four men were diagnosed *varioloid* and none died. However, 28 of the 47 clear cases of small pox died, 10 of whom were prisoners of war.

The differences between the effects of measles and small pox are so marked that it is hardly surprising that the latter required much longer hospitalization. To recover from measles or rubeola took on average 11 days. The great majority of the cases, and all of the shorter stays, were in 1862 in Wilmington. This is to be expected in that measles, in its various forms, was one of the diseases that swept through early training camps. By 1863, most veterans were immune to the disease. On the other hand, the strong majority of small pox cases occurred in the last two years of the war. The average hospital stay for men who recovered from small pox was 35 days.

EXAMPLE: William Robinson[31] was treated twice for measles (rubeola) in February and March 1862; he must have contracted malaria for he was hospitalized in May 1862 for acute rheumatism and then restricted to quarters until 10 June 1862; December 1862, he was given sick furlough for 40 days; in February 1863, he was admitted to a hospital in Richmond with a heart condition (anasarca); upon release he was declared unfit for duty and, therefore, detailed as a nurse from late February 1863 until the end of July 1863 when he contracted small pox; he survived small pox and was again detailed as a nurse from 22 August 1863 through June 1864; on 12 July 1864 he was captured either with his company or at the hospital; he died in captivity of acute bronchitis on 30 January 1865.

Malaria

> *"The doctor says [I have] the rheumatism but I am in hopes that he is mistaken. He put a ... grate big blister on my back but I don't think that it done any good only it taken the skin off and you may guess whether that done me much good or naught."*
> —B.C. Jackson, September 1862

The term malaria never appears in the documents of the Civil War, though there are some references to malarial fevers. Rather, physicians and surgeons diagnosed according to the nature and recurrence of malarial chills and fevers. Thus, men were hospitalized or furloughed for ague, congestive fever, congestive chill, intermittent fevers, third-day fevers, fourth-day fevers, and acute rheumatism which we believe referred to the intense joint pain often caused by malaria. Altogether there were 125 episodes resulting from malaria: 51 of recurring or simple intermittent fever; three of third-day fevers; four of fourth-day fevers; 67 of acute rheumatism or furloughs to convalesce from same.

It is difficult to measure the devastation of malaria among the men of the 30th. On the one hand, only two deaths are attributed to the disease and one of those, congestive chill, could have been another disease. Only the most severe, intractable cases tended to be hospitalized. The longest stays were 329 days, 241 days, and 189 days, and the shortest one day. However, of the 26 hospital stays less than one week, 24 were in the spring of 1862 in Wilmington, raising some suspicion about the diagnoses. The average hospital stay for malaria, taking all cases, was 32 days.[32] D. McLeod, a friend of the Jackson family of Moore County, North Carolina, wrote on 2 December 1862 that he had been sick with "fever & chills" since 1 October. He managed to stop them several times by taking quinine, but they kept coming back so he went to the hospital in Lynchburg, Virginia. The doctors there would stop the chills but they continued to return. On 2 December, he reported that he had had no chills for a week and hoped he was cured. He intended to ask for a furlough or even a discharge having done no duty since he arrived in Virginia and expected to do none for the rest of the year.[33]

The weakening of men and the amount of time men were unable to function due to malaria was enormous and certainly under-represented by the data. The editors of *MSHWR* reported that many men in the Union Army did not bother to hospitalize themselves for recurring chills and only came in for quinine to lessen the intensity. It is most likely that the men of the 30th reported even less for they surely had less access to quinine. In the fall of 1861, Louis McLeod wrote to his wife about the number of fevers in camp and that the company captain had been confined to his tent for days suffering from malaria. "I never saw a man have a harder ague than he did."[34] None of these cases were admitted to a hospital or show up in records. Among Union troops, there was a dramatic spike in malarial episodes in August or September of each year. In the 30th North Carolina, they would seem to have three annual spikes: in the spring when the first batch of mosquitoes hatched, a second in mid-summer and a third in November. This last spike may well correspond to the Union Army's experience in that it is predominately "rheumatism" which would be following attacks of chills and fevers a month or so earlier (Figure 20).

EXAMPLE: Alexander Denson[35] was sent home sick in October 1861; contracted malaria in March 1862; gastritis in May 1862; diagnosed with acute rheumatism in November 1862; admitted to Chimborazo in March 1863 with debility; April 1863 was in Huguenot Hospital in Richmond with acute diarrhea until June; was captured at Kelly's Ford in November 1863 and admitted to prison hospital in May 1864 with small pox.

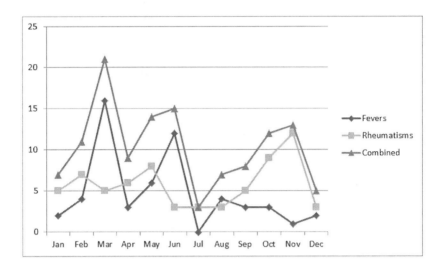

Figure 20. Malarial Episodes by Month

Typhoid Fever

Many different diagnoses were given for typhoid fever: continuing fever, common continuing fever, bilious fever, fever, typhoid pneumonia, and of course *febris typhoides*. Whatever it was called it was the absolute bane of the 30th North Carolina. There were 210 episodes, over 10 percent of the total, involving 160 individuals, nearly 18 percent of all patients and accounting for 81 deaths. Six of the incidences were diagnosed as camp fever or typhus. Typhus had been one of the deadliest killers in European wars of the 18th and 19th centuries but for some reason played very little part in the Civil War in either army. We will lump those six incidences with typhoid.

There was great variation in how long men were hospitalized for typhoid depending on severity of the attack. The longest stay was 145 days by a man who was at the time a prisoner of war and was hospitalized by his captors. The shortest stays were one or two days, mostly concentrated in early 1862 at the main Wilmington, North Carolina, hospital. The average length of hospital stay for all typhoid suffers was 62 days. It is very possible that those early Wilmington diagnoses were either very mild cases or a different disease altogether. We have, therefore, done a second analysis dropping the stays of less than one week, almost all in the spring of 1862, and three excessively long furloughs for typhoid—the men may have simply delayed returning. This gives an average stay of 36½ days.

Typhoid, contracted often from drinking water with the pathogen, could attack any time of the year. Only December and January, when men were in better quarters with well water available, saw lower numbers (Figure 21). There is considerable variation among *Salmonella Typhi*, the bacteria that causes typhoid, and as a result humans do not develop immunity to the disease and can suffer with it several times.

EXAMPLE: Neverson Batchelor[36] contracted typhoid fever in Wilmington in early June 1862; he was given a 30-day furlough to recover, returning to duty around 13 July 1862; September 1862, he was admitted to Chimborazo with acute diarrhea; he was then given a 30-day sick furlough which he overstayed, going AWOL until early February 1863; he was captured at Kelly's Ford on 7 November 1863; admitted to a prison hospital 2 January 1864 with small pox; and died of small pox while a POW on 7 February 1864.

EXAMPLE: Alfred Mashburn[37] was furloughed home sick during December 1861; he was admitted to a hospital in Richmond on 23

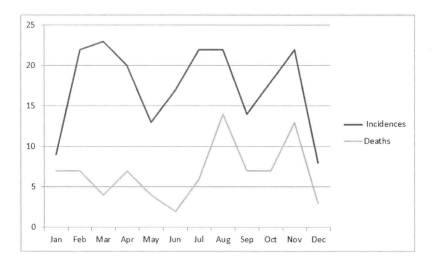

Figure 21. Typhoid Fever Incidences by Month

June 1862 with typhoid fever, not being released until after the Seven Days Campaign was complete; he was wounded at Antietam, returning to duty on 15 November 1862; on Christmas day 1862, admitted to Chimborazo with pneumonia; May 1863, he was absent sick; the two months of July and August 1863, he was at Chimborazo suffering acute diarrhea and acute rheum; from 1 September 1863 until January 1864, he was given sick furlough; in April 1864, he was admitted to a hospital with acute bronchitis; end of April to 1 November 1864 he was detailed as a nurse; he then vanishes from the records, doubtless slipping away home.

Other Infectious Diseases

> *"[after the amputation his] system proved not strong enough to throw out the 'pus' or inflammation; and this, mingling with the blood produced that most fatal of all diseases,* pyaemia, *from which no one ever recovers."*
>
> —Phoebe Yates Pember

This category is large because it includes rheum and catarrhus, 133 incidences, involving 121 men. These two diseases were probably mild cases of typhoid, influenza or some other disease which produced copious amounts of nasal discharge and mucous. Catarrhus was diagnosed 47 times and acute rheum 19 times. There were no deaths, which reinforces the view that they were mild episodes of more serious diseases. There were 29 cases of probable hepatitis: acute hepatitis 13, icterus 14 and jaundice 2.[38] Hospital stays ranged from two to 53 days and averaged 20 days. The worst killer was "brain fever" or meningitis, which killed eight men. In addition, there were 10 cases of cholera, one of conjunctivitis, one of diphtheria, 13 of *parotitis* or mumps, two deaths from blood poisoning, two cases of scarlet fever with one death and one scrofulous ulcer of the leg. These diseases are very under-represented for the first part of the war. Louis McLeod wrote that dozens in his company alone suffered from mumps in the fall of 1861. Outbreaks were so common that men were simply confined to quarters and no report was made.

EXAMPLE: One of the more unfortunate men was William Autry.[39] Private Autry spent the first months of 1862 at home on sick furlough; on 4 May 1862, he was admitted to Wilmington General Hospital with *pleuritis*; mid–May 1862, he was readmitted to Wilmington for acute hepatitis; at the end of May, his diagnosis was changed to "*rheum acuta*"; late in August 1862, he was admitted to a hospital in Richmond with acute diarrhea; he was captured during the battle of Antietam and exchanged at once; he died on 18 December 1862 of pneumonia.

Non-Infectious Diseases

> "*The surgeons feared to remove this mass, as it might be connected with the nerves of the foot, and lock-jaw might ensue.*"
> —Phoebe Yates Pember

This very large category contained 227 incidences affecting 187 men. The most common notations were *debilitas* 115 men and "unfit for duty" 56 men. Add to that, two men who were "convalescing" and one who died of "exhaustion." This diagnosis represents men whose health was so weak that they were incapable of performing duty. On average, they were hospitalized for 50 days. However, some of the very short stays were followed by debility furloughs.

The remaining 53 diagnoses were anemia six, asthma two, *constipates* four, deftness two, *delirium tremens* one, dyspepsia 14, gangrene two (both deaths), *hemeralopia* one, hernia one, lumbago two, neuralgia six, *nyctalopia* one, sciatica two, *scorbutus*[40] or scurvy nine.

Conditions of Unknown Cause

This small group of 27 incidences involving 26 men occurred early in the war—all but four incidences by December 1962. This would indicate that these afflictions were diagnosed differently later in the war when surgeons had more experience. Two men suffered abscesses, two from *epistaxis* (nose bleeds), six from gastritis, three from *haematemesis*,[41] two from *hemositis* (blood clots), two with spinal pain, one with ear pain, four from *otorrhoea* (probably perforated ear drum), two from phlebitis, one "dead w admitted," and one from an unidentifiable condition called "*hydrothrus*" which must have been collection of fluid someplace in the body.

Hospitals

There were an enormous number of hospitals operating in North Carolina and Virginia where the 30th was billeted or fought. Richmond alone had well over a hundred.[42] Every town of any size on a railroad had hospitals, and some like Charlottesville and Lynchburg in Virginia became major depots for the sick and wounded. The hospitals ranged from as small as a couple of rooms in a private house to as large as the massive Chimborazo complex on the edge of Richmond.

While it is doubtless true that surgeons and hospital staff did the best they could to care for men, ignorance and lack of resources made many hospitals little better than death traps. Surgeons who tried to get the convalescing furloughed for recovery were often frustrated by the army's need to get men back into the lines quickly. The army also feared, for good reason, that if the men were furloughed home they might not return. Surgeon A.F. Magnon furloughed Private Willis N. Bowlin of Company D for 30 days to recuperate from a wound in the right arm suffered at Chancellorsville. The furlough was canceled by military authorities who objected to sending the wounded home. Magnon protested this decision by writing, "In the opinion of the undersigned wounded soldiers who merely require time [*sic*] for the recovery ought not to be confined in a city where variola and encephalitis are endemic."[43]

The only hospital that offered much chance of good treatment was Chimborazo. This complex was constructed following the observations of Florence Nightingale on the horrors of British and French hospitals during the Crimean War. The buildings were airy, with many windows and room around each bed. Fortunate indeed were those men who were admitted to Chimborazo.[44] Most men ended up in other hospitals. In 1863, there was an attempt made to group men in hospitals by state. As a result men of the 30th North Carolina were most often admitted in Richmond to Mount Jackson and General Hospitals #22 and #24. When admitted to Chimborazo, they were often transferred after one or two days to a hospital designated mostly for North Carolinians. There is no indication that medical care varied from hospital to hospital. More likely the grouping of men by states reflects the weak unity of the Confederacy and efforts to force states to shoulder responsibility for their own men. In some cases, however, men were assigned regardless of state. This was evident at Howard's Grove dedicated to small pox and General Hospital #13 used for mental illness. Men who needed a very long recovery period and who could travel would often be sent to Wilmington, Charlotte, Winston, Raleigh or Tarboro.

Even if a man could receive sick furlough from the hospital, many were too weak to leave and were, thus, doomed to stay. Willis Goodin was in this situation in July 1862. He had been admitted to the hospital with typhoid fever on 20 July 1862. He asked that his parents come to Richmond and take him home as he was too weak to come on his own.[45] Willis died on 30 August 1862 of typhoid and chronic dysentery.

It is unlikely that a single man in the regiment survived the war without at least one or two serious attacks by some disease. Inept doctors and surgeons combined with no understanding of how disease spread ensured this and the high number of deaths. The situation was exacerbated by malnutrition and inadequate clothes in winter. Food shortages and lack of clothing will be discussed in the next chapter.

10

Starvation and Desertion

*"it is a snowing here to day in a hury & it is power-
ful cold we are in a field & little wood to burn & nothing to eat"*
—A.F. Harrington, January 1864

When does scarcity become famine? At what point did the Confederate Army, and the 30th North Carolina in particular, cross from
hunger to near starvation? Was there a point at which dissatisfaction
and resentment became so strong that the ability of the regiment to
fight was impaired? Probably there was not a particular week or month
when hunger and despair became all-consuming. The reality was that
over the course of three years from April 1862 to April 1865 the situation of the 30th North Carolina with regard to food and supplies went
steadily from poor to unbearable. The very slowness of the decline
insured that the men would, for the most part, keep fighting and survive. It was much like the urban myth that a frog in a pot of water
slowly heating will adapt to each degree of increase even to the point
of being boiled rather than jumping.

Food shortages sapped the strength of the men of the 30th in
two ways. First, there was the obvious difficulty of insufficient calo-
ries to maintain health and energy. Second, unit strength was reduced
as increasing numbers of men came to see desertion as the only way
to survive. Some surrendered to the Union Army to get food. Others slipped away toward home. Those who fled home in the winters
of 1862 or 1863 sometimes returned in the spring, and the regiment's
strength would rebound a bit. Those who left in late 1864 or early 1865
never returned and were permanently lost to the regiment.

Food supply was truly adequate only for the first six months
after the 30th North Carolina was formed. Even then, from October

10. Starvation and Desertion

1861–May 1862, men relied on food from home—easy since the regiment was stationed in the vicinity of Wilmington—to improve the sufficient but unappetizing victuals supplied by Confederacy or state. As noted above, Louis McLeod wrote his wife that they ate well except for not having molasses. By April 1862, his comments on food shifted. The food was described as poor. They got little to eat but pickled [salted or corned] pork and that the fattest sort. Once in a while, he wrote, they got a quarter of old, tough beef that must have been a steer used for pulling a wagon. They mostly ate the pork and corn bread, of which they had plenty. The officers' mess had very little wheat bread, and coffee was but a memory. Unlike enlisted men, officers and non-commissioned officers had to pay cooks from their own funds. There was considerable resentment at both the quality of the food and at having to pay.[1]

From the beginning of the war, the men suffered from inadequate supplies of all kinds, not just food. In April 1862, Louis McLeod wrote to his wife that they were very cold and were only permitted to carry one or two blankets. He had one and his friend H.J. McNeill gave him a second. At night to keep warm, the men had partners that they stayed close to for warmth. His partner was Horrace Morrison.[2] "We ly close together when the knights is cold."[3]

The inadequacy of supply was evident from the earliest months of actual combat. Not only did the regiment fight several intense battles in Maryland in the autumn of 1862 culminating at Antietam, but it did so on very short rations. Lieutenant Ardrey noted that they survived for four days on one day's rations.[4] No rations were available on 20 September, and Ardrey ate only three ears of green corn. On 28 September, Ardrey noted the boys spent the day shooting squirrels, for food rather than sport one would assume. William Sillers wrote to his sister two weeks after Antietam that the regiment had "done a great deal of cruel marching, been very much starved, and fought two hard battles in Maryland."[5] They had nothing to eat but beef without salt on 14 October though the sutler brought in some cider, honey, butter and apples.[6]

In the winter of 1862, the 30th was part of Jackson's "Foot Cavalry." They were constantly on the march in the Shenandoah Valley, often through heavy snow. Even a well-fed and well-equipped army would have found serving under Jackson difficult. The Foot Cavalry was neither. "It is not one or two who are without shoes and half-clad but it is the greater part of every company in our regiment who are in this condition ... men who have been without [shoes and clothes] for months."[7]

Diary entries by William Ardrey reflect this increased misery. On 26 January 1863, he wrote that rations were very scarce and 10 men deserted from Company I. The next day, 27 January 1863, 16 men deserted from his company.

By late March 1863, the daily ration was only 4 oz. of meat and 18 oz. of flour.[8] Colonel Parker observed in a letter that the slaves on his plantation ate considerably better. Mrs. Parker had sold some hams, and the colonel suggested that she reduce the slaves to 3½ lbs. of pork per week. She had plenty of beef and other food. That should let her send some to the army. "If the soldiers, your husband and brothers, can live upon ¼ lb. per day, surely the negroes can do so likewise. This is a subject which I am afraid the people have not properly considered."[9] The only sure supply was the ¼ lb. of bacon. Colonel Parker wrote later in the month, "rations of the men is short: ¼ lbs. of bacon is a small allowance for a soldier, for an entire day; particularly as they get nothing else."[10] Parker again urged his wife in May to reduce rations to the slaves to ½ lb. per day and send some bacon for his men.[11]

Any time the men could forage for food, they ate better for a while. In April 1863, the regiment took advantage of the spring shad run which in those days was obviously still strong in the rivers around Richmond and for several days, shad was the main food in the mess.[12]

That the regular supply of food was not improved is clear from a letter written by B.C. Jackson. He had been detailed to a squad of cooks (he had been very sick and probably not capable of real duty) which had to prepare and take rations four miles each day to the regiment which was on picket duty down the Rappahannock River. For five days, beginning 24 April 1863, Jackson's squad transported food. He recognized that it would have been better to take several days' rations each trip, but since rations were in such short supply, the cooks could never draw more than one day at a time. He did write that things were quiet down river. He saw three Yankees across the river one day, and one was fishing.[13]

Two weeks after the Battle of Chancellorsville, Lt. A.A. Jackson, B.C. Jackson's older brother, wrote his family about how they had fared in the battle and commented, "[W]e are faring tolerable well at this time on our small rations."[14]

Desertion, because of starvation or other discontent, was already a serious problem in the spring of 1863. B.C. Jackson wrote his sister on 23 March 1863 that the night before 50 men had deserted from the brigade, eight from the 30th and one from his company.[15] Jackson assumed that they left because of resentment over not getting enough to eat. He admitted that the rations were "mity short." One week later, Private D.C. Shaw[16] wrote Effie Jackson that when he arrived back at camp after a furlough home, men were running away from the regiment every day but he thought Company H would stay.[17] The brigade response was to take two men of the 30th, recaptured after running, and administer 30 lashes each on bare backs.[18] Desertions continued throughout the summer. Rufus Stallings wrote that nearly every night "some of our men run away. But it is some who are not worth much, men who hardly ever actually go into battle. But they try and get good men to go with them."[19]

It is certain that during the Civil War, North Carolina troops were prone to large scale desertion. In fact, desertion of men from many states was a problem for the Confederate Army. Lee and others complained that North Carolina was guilty of by far the highest rate of desertion. The accusation was continued in official reports after the war and then by historians. The question historians disagreed upon was why so many Carolinians deserted. The traditional view has been that they deserted primarily for two reasons: need to assist their families at home, especially in planting and harvest seasons; and disillusion with the war and with the Confederate government.[20]

It is likely that the high numbers repeated by historians in the past were grossly inflated. Few North Carolinians were high in the Confederate government or army, and strong peace movements in the state and initial reluctance to secession hardly endeared the state to the Confederate government or army. Richard Reid wrote that Davis, Lee and many Virginians in the Confederate Army distrusted and disliked North Carolina. In a masterful, statistical study written in 1981, Reid revised the number of North Carolina deserters downward from 23,694 to about 14,000 and reduced the number of officers deserting by 90 percent.[21] Even 14,000 represents heavy desertion, though in line with other states. The question remains: why did the men flee?

Recent historians have revised thinking about the reasons for desertion. Aaron Sheehan-Dean reports high desertion rates among Virginia soldiers, especially in the fall of 1862 and as 1864 turned into 1865. He agrees that in some places desertion may have reflected abandonment of the Confederacy but insists, "This was not the case in Virginia."[22] Even if he is correct, does that speak to North Carolinians?

In the 1990s, several historians and sociologists revisited the question of motivations for desertions using a 10-percent sample of the 120,000 North Carolina soldiers, including some from the 30th. Katherine Giuffre reached some of the most interesting conclusions.[23] After rejecting a number of hypotheses such as cowardice and rich versus poor, she shows strong evidence for heads of household deserting at harvest[24] and for desertion as a political statement against the Confederate government. Her arguments and evidence are convincing. "The poor farmers and farm laborers of North Carolina resisted the war and resisted the Confederate Army not by mutiny, which would have been suicidal, but by desertion. The soldiers of the North Carolina Confederate Army resisted the Confederacy through individual, rather than collective, acts."[25] Desertions by men in the 30th fit her pattern.

By the spring of 1863, desertion was so serious a problem for the 30th that some loyal men had to be detailed home to hunt and capture deserters and collect conscripts who had not reported. On 13 March 1863, J.L. Cox[26] and James Deaton, both of Company H, were so detailed.[27] In addition to regular pay, this duty paid $.40 per day wages, $.75 per day for rations and a $30 bounty for each deserter returned. It was by such an officer from the 32nd North Carolina that Private Bennett Crumpler (Company I) was apprehended and returned to the regiment in November 1863.[28] Before mid–December 1863, Private Crumpler had again deserted never to be heard from again. Charles L. Goebel (Company B) was worth even more. His captor was paid a $50 bounty. Goebel was a skilled mechanic and had been assigned to the Richmond armory from March 1862 until June 1863 when he went AWOL. After his arrest in August 1863, he managed to disappear again and never returned to the armory or regiment.[29]

In the spring of 1863, for one last time the men ate better for a few days. Food arrived from families back home. On 16 May 1863, Ardrey wrote that 14 large boxes from home arrived for Company K and they feasted. Temporarily, even the commissaries did better and on 30 May 1863, J.W. Brassfield wrote his parents that they were eating well and had plenty of meat.[30] This relative wealth lasted through June. On 25 June 1863, daily rations reached 18 oz. flour and 8 oz. bacon "[w]hich does very well for a soldier."[31] Food became even more plentiful for the remainder of June 1863 as the 30th moved into Maryland and Pennsylvania and could requisition food from prosperous farms.

By the autumn of 1863, food and morale were lower than ever. The brigade command decided it was necessary to take extreme measures against desertion. On 16 September 1863, Rufus Stallings wrote his fiancée that he had seen a terrible sight. One of the brigade was shot for running away. All had to march onto a field and line up to watch. The man was tied to a stob but it looked like he didn't much care for he just knelt down at his place like nothing was the matter.[32]

By the winter of 1863, the men were increasingly despondent. They were barely fed and clothed by the Confederacy. If there had been no food from home arriving, it is hard to imagine they would have survived at all. In addition, they were mostly camped in areas of Virginia that were so devastated by war that there was little food to steal or confiscate.

Finally, they were being paid in Confederate paper currency which was becoming nearly worthless as inflation soared. Lack of confidence in a Confederate victory meant that many refused to accept the money at all.

It wasn't just conscripts and Quakers who were turning against the war. Men who had volunteered with such furor in 1861, and who maintained throughout 1862 that victory was possible with more sacrifice, no longer were optimistic. They tried to keep younger brothers and relatives out of the war. Lt. A.A. Jackson's younger brother Garry took a job at a mill to gain an exemption from the draft. The lieutenant was concerned that Garry might not be clear because he had not been at the mill very long. His concern grew for the enrolling officer for the county was the former captain of Company H, William Swann. "I expect he will bare down on him as he is my brother. I being an officer in his old company and helped to turn him out of office."[33]

Even in times of scarceness men found ways to celebrate occasions and get some pleasure. In early December 1863, Private Pegram[34] was elected lieutenant in Company B. By way of celebration he treated the company to a barrel of apples and invited William Ardrey to join in.[35] At Christmas 1863, two sergeants in Company K, Taylor Lee[36] and John Black,[37] went out in the countryside and somehow found some brandy, cakes, apples and some other delights. The officers and non-commissioned officers at least celebrated with the bounty.[38]

The year ended in utter despair for the 30th following the devastation of the regiment at Kelly's Ford on 19 November. On 5 December 1863, there were only 21 present in company D for 28 had been taken prisoner at Kelly's Ford.[39]

Even as the men struggled on, for men of property trouble was appearing from yet another direction. They were being paid in Confederate currency. Lieutenant-Colonel Sillers asked his brother-in-law, Doctor Holmes, to collect some debts owed him and to pay some of his notes that were due. However, he requested care be taken in the process for "Confederate money is not a legal tender and some may prefer the notes to the money."[40] "Find out which of my creditors will accept that money before collecting too much of it for me," he added. Two weeks later Sillers mentioned the subject again but with more panic. He had been told that people were paying off debts as quickly as possible with Confederate currency. Now he asked the doctor to pay off what he owes and "have no scruples about it."[41]

William Ardrey related in his diary that he barely averted disaster with Confederate money. His brother and the executor of his father's estate wanted to sell the family land for Confederate money and then invest the money in Confederate bonds. Ardrey and his sister prevailed, and the land was not sold.[42]

During 1864, supplies dwindled even more. On 31 March 1864, George K. Harrell,[43] functioning as Assistant Quartermaster of the 30th, received from Buckner Williams, now Quartermaster of Ramseur's Brigade, the following: 345 cords of wood; 880 lbs. corn; 440 lbs. hay; 785 lbs. straw; 77 pairs of shoes; 58 pairs of pants; 13 jackets; 34 caps; 13 pairs of socks; 31 lbs. sole leather; 7 lbs. upper leather; 30 quires writing paper; one blank book; four skillets; two camp kettles; three mush pans; two water buckets; one quart tar; 15 lbs. wagon grease; and one packing box. This was for approximately 400 men, officers and animals. What we can't know is how long this was expected to last and how often other supplies might have been made available.[44]

A.F. Harrington wrote to John A. McDonald, who was home on

leave, in January 1864 about conditions, "it is a snowing here to day in a hury & it is powerful cold we are in a field & little wood to burn & nothing to eat We drawd baken to day one quarter of a pound for one days rashon but we has to do three days on that You no we fare bad here now James Rogers[45] brought me a fine box but it is all gone now & you may guess how hungry I am."[46] At the same time Rufus Stallings commented how he "hated to see men barefoot in the cold."[47]

One month later John A. McDonald was back with the regiment—rations were even shorter: "On the scene of rations we suffer. We get enough of corn bread to do for bread but we get only one pound of meat per week. The daily ration of meat is too small to divide, it has to be eaten at one meal. We sometimes get a little molasses & a little rice but in such small quantities they do but little good. I think the commissaries are to blame a good deal for our stinted rations. The men are getting a great deal in boxes from home. If it were not for this I do not see how they would get along."[48] Those who did not get a box or who were not fortunate enough to be given a share from a comrade did suffer. James L. Green wrote in April, "We get one quarter of a pound of bacon, [and a] pound and a quarter of corn meal and little sugar and coffee and rice per day. I am very often hungry."[49]

In March 1864, James L. Green described a 20-mile march in constant freezing rain and snow. Days later, his legs "hurts me very bad yet." He then related that nearly one-third of the pickets from the brigade "went over to the Yankey," including his best friend, Hunter,[50] and one more man from Company H.[51]

Things did not improve in the summer though battle increased. Joseph Goodin said on 28 June 1864 that he had been in line of battle for the last two weeks with nothing to eat but bread & bacon.[52]

In the winter after the failure of Early's invasion of Maryland—the third time the 30th crossed the Potomac—the regiment was back near Petersburg in winter quarters having marched two days through the snow from the Shenandoah Valley. The supplies were no better. On Christmas Eve 1864: "We get no more food than in the valey. A man can eat all at one time what he gets for a days ration & not have a large meal at that. I did draw shoes but have nearly wore them out."[53]

By early 1864, so many men were deserting in the face of near famine that army commanders resorted to more drastic steps. The decision was made to execute a few deserters as examples.[54] On 29 April

1864, the brigade was assembled and three men from the brigade were marched into a field, tied to stakes and shot. The executions made a strong impression of the men of the 30th. Rather than deter desertions, the men seem to have felt the action cruel and unjustified. Young Joseph Goodin described his reaction to the execution. "I never felt so sad in my life. The guns fierd[,] tha trimbled and the blud run down their socks. Tha were berried in the cold field."[55] James L. Green described the same execution to his wife. They were marched to the field with a band playing, a chaplain prayed, the men knelt, were tied to stakes, blindfolded and shot. "It looked like they was shot most all to pieces. I never want to see another such a sight. It seemed like I could not stand it."[56] William Ardrey noted in his diary it was "one of the saddest scenes that I have ever witnessed in my life."[57] The brigade resorted to many kinds of punishment for desertion and cowardice in battle: wearing barrel jackets; ball and chain; hard labor; and forced to ride wooden horses.[58]

It was not only soldiers who were abandoning the war. Many civilians were ready to end the struggle. From 1863 on, a peace movement in North Carolina sought to take the state out of the Confederacy, but not necessarily back into the Union.[59] A.F. Harrington asked his brother John Harrington about the peace movement in the summer of 1863. The army was full of rumors that North Carolina was going back into the Union. Sergeant Harrington hated the war and would like to see it end. However, he said "go with any body else but Abe."[60] One month later Sergeant Harrington was still thinking about the peace movement. "I am tired of this ware but I don't want to live under Old Abe But I fere some times we will have to do it."[61]

In the spring of 1864, discontent and anger over the war was so intense in North Carolina that Confederate authorities feared the peace movement led by William W. Holden would succeed.[62] A. Jackson wrote a long letter from the army on the subject. Some in his family apparently were much taken with the peace movement. One said she would as soon see Davis dead as Yankees. Jackson refutes all this in Biblical terms. For his part he will stick with Davis and "Uncle Bobby Lee."[63]

By the end of 1864, the Confederate Army was near collapse. To have mutinied and refused to fight would have been suicidal. The number of men deserting, however, increased dramatically. Many, citing grossly insufficient food, wrote families that they planned to leave and would do so at the first opportunity.[64] This was very evident among recent conscripts who were unwilling to be in the army and looked for every opportunity to desert. Letters from John J. Armfield to his wife reflect this attitude in very stark terms.[65]

Armfield[66] was a 35-year-old, married Quaker who was conscripted with other men in Guildford County and assigned to Company C of the 30th North Carolina. The men had no desire to fight and despised the army and those who supported the war. Armfield commented on one doctor from home who was full of "sesech" venom. His letters to his wife are filled with vague plans to desert at the first opportunity. He and others he refers to were restrained from desertion not because of the examples of execution, but solely because the loyal troops on picket and guard would shoot them if they tried. It is a clear mark of the desperation of the Confederate government that such men were forced into the ranks. In addition, some of them probably should have been rejected for reasons of health. One of the group, named Phillip, fell sick with pneumonia upon arrival and died before he could be officially entered on the regimental roster.

The men were so hungry and desperate that they began to openly express their anger to officers and even generals. John L. Shearin[67] of Company B in his reminiscences written after the war related that he was with the unit under Jubal Early when it reached Washington, D.C. During the retreat back to Virginia in September, he was wounded at Winchester and given a 40-day furlough. He returned to the Valley and Early's command in November. One day when Early rode past, the men all cried out "bread, bread." Early glared at them and shouted back "remember Cedar Creek damn you."[68]

In November 1864, the regiment went back to Petersburg and in 1865 was put into the trenches defending the city. This meant there was no real opportunity to desert. Armfield's letters are increasingly unhappy. He described himself as "desperate" on 10 March 1865.

The starkness of terrible deficiencies was clear in the report submitted by an inspector for Cox's brigade on 25 February 1865.[69] The regiment had five officers and 176 men present with three officers and 49 men absent without leave. The report noted that the regiment suffered from grave clothing deficiencies as well as lacking bayonets, scabbards and cartridge boxes. Deficiencies included 67 overcoats,

275 coats, 200 trousers, 205 shirts, 120 pairs of shoes, 125 stockings, 46 blankets, 200 knapsacks, 160 canteens and 50 tents. It is clear that the great majority of the regiment was inadequately clothed as well as inadequately fed.

The last letter this author found from a member of the regiment was dated 23 March 1865. J.J. Goodin begs his family to send food and write more.[70] What began as a great adventure was ending as famine and death.

It is assumed by historians that the Army of Northern Virginia was near starvation by the spring of 1865. Nothing in the documents relating to the 30th would at all disagree with that assumption. The real question is why they fought on so long. Clifford Dowdey and other historians have seen the answer as a willingness to follow Lee so long as he led.[71] Perhaps so, but what was more important, as always with fighting men, was their loyalty to each other. After the fall of Petersburg, not even that strong bond would hold them in the field. In the first week of April, as the army retreated towards Appomattox, the regiment could count only 243 men and officers. By the time Lee met with Grant on 9 April, 14 percent (34 men) had vanished and 25 percent (62 men) had gone over to the enemy. By May, there would have been no men left to surrender. One man who had been with the 30th since the fall of 1861 and who had served faithfully was Sergeant A.F. Harrington. He was at the end of his endurance. "I am tired of this mud. Ware & mud is tiresome. Our men are deserting continualy, Some to the yanks & some home John. I don't think I ever will desert But my head feels mitely like a deserters dose some times."[72] He concluded his letter by saying that if he heard Sherman had reached Moore County, North Carolina, he would desert at that instant and return home. Sherman reached central North Carolina about the same time that the 30th surrendered. Harrington may have arrived back in Moore County just as the first Union soldiers occupied it.

Perhaps there were soldiers who lamented the surrender or who called out to Lee that they were ready to fight on. Such has been stated in many accounts of the surrender. More likely the truth is the few men remaining in the field must have agreed with R.M. Crumpler[73] who wrote in his diary, "[A]ll were greatly relieved that the war was over and we were alive."[74]

Conclusion

What conclusions can be drawn about the men of the 30th North Carolina? That they were on the wrong side of history is obvious. That they fought, whatever their motivations, to preserve the abhorrent system of enslavement of their fellow humans cannot be denied. Even so, they deserve our pity and some respect, even if grudging.

First, it is impossible to know the volunteers and not admire their sense of patriotism for their state and homes; their strong sense of honor to complete a terrible task; and strong loyalty to their fellow soldiers. The majority suffered privation, wounds and terror without quitting. Most of those captured in 1863 and early 1864 remained loyal to their comrades and rejected Union offers of pardon and freedom if they would join the U.S. Army. Only in late 1864 and 1865 did this tenacious loyalty begin to break down under near starvation conditions and an increasing belief that the war could not be won and further fighting would serve only to produce more useless suffering and death.

Second, after the initial outburst of volunteers to repulse what they saw as invasion, the great majority of men who joined the regiment were forced in against their will through the draft, often at gunpoint. These conscripted men probably had opposed secession and certainly did not wish to war against the Union. These men especially deserve our pity and respect.

Third, it is very clear reading letters written by the men of the 30th North Carolina that the old myths of the Civil War, both of the North and of the South, are based, at best, on very fragile bases. The men of the 30th North Carolina had little or no sense of being "Southerners." They saw themselves first as being of a particular county and then as being of North Carolina. Almost never did a man call himself

Conclusion

a Confederate or a Southerner. The Confederacy was not a true union, rather a very loose coalition of states whose citizens often were suspicious of each other. Localism extended even to the county level. Regiments could only depend for help on counties from which they were recruited and then only from certain individuals.

The men of the 30th did not dislike the lieutenant and major generals under whom they served. However, there is no sign that they held them in great veneration, that they were willing to follow them blindly. Only two times in all these letters was General Lee mentioned—once that he was preferable to the 1864 North Carolina peace movement and once that he had been viewed and was a handsome man.

It is difficult not to feel anger on behalf of the men, volunteers and conscripts, for all the betrayals they suffered. Many of these men were probably opposed to secession in early 1861. Governor Ellis and his allies in the State Assembly took North Carolina out of the Union and into rebellion by using devious methods to prevent the people from speaking. Secessionists, in alliance with the rich planters of the state, used men like those of the 30th to fight to defend their right to own slaves by cloaking the war as one against invasion. Of course, there were planters like Francis Parker and William Sillers who placed themselves in the line of battle, but one suspects that the majority paid substitutes, found reasons to leave the army early or hid behind the exemption that let a white man supervising 20 or more slaves stay out. Even Parker left by the end of 1864, much to the anger of his men. "Coln Parker has bin retired & left us All the big men are getting out of the ware as fast as they can."[1]

Finally, these men were betrayed by their own generals and the government of the Confederacy in 1863–1864. It was clear to the men after the disaster at Gettysburg that victory was probably impossible. Even planters, like William Sillers, who did not ask others to fight his fight, wrote his sister, "It seems as if we are just on the threshold of ruin."[2] It is understandable that Davis, Lee and others were not willing to give up so soon. There was a slim chance of success if the war grew too painful for the North. The leaders faced a good chance of personal loss and punishment if the South lost. Letters from men of the 30th, written in the second half of 1864 and into 1865, are filled with despair. Given the lack of food and supplies, large scale desertion and strong anti–Confederate feeling at home, many men of the 30th saw no hope for victory. Yet, Davis and Lee fought on. Davis even wanted the army to scatter and form irregular units and continue to fight after Appomattox and Bentonville. By continuing the war for over a year and a half after Gettysburg, whether it was to protect slavery, themselves or some sense of honor, these men succeeded only in bringing more death and destruction to the entire South. For men of the 30th, the war had become an all-devouring monster and, when speaking frankly, they drew few distinctions between the armies. "May the Lord have mercy on us if either army gets close to ur homes for I no how they tare up things."[3]

One of the myths of the "Lost Cause" has been the reluctance of the men to quit at Appomattox.[4] Whether it is a picture of common soldiers crying and telling Lee, "No, don't, we can fight on," or some grizzled colonel saying "We'll go home, make a harvest and then go at them again," it was all as Sherman said about war—it was moonshine. These men, brave, loyal, strong were finally at the end of endurance. Fifty to 60 per week were going over to the enemy or melting into the countryside. By the 7th of May, Lee would have surrendered little more than his staff and himself.

After the war and surrender, many in the South sentimentalized Appomattox. The men of the 30th North Carolina did not. Their feeling was best expressed by Private Crumpler in his diary. "Thank God this war is over."

Appendix:
Present or Accounted For

A full-strength Confederate regiment consisted of 1,000 men and officers. The 30th North Carolina never achieved that level and only approached it in the late spring of 1862. The unit first went into combat in the Seven Days Campaign at approximately 75 percent and never saw combat at full strength. To determine the actual strength of the regiment with high certainty is difficult. Many personnel records were not preserved or remained in private hands after the war and are, therefore, not accessible to the historian. Furthermore, as the war progressed records were kept more sporadically and haphazardly.

The most accurate and straightforward way to determine numbers should be to process the data on men found in *North Carolina Troops*, Vol. VIII, pp. 314–423.[1] The editors attempted to compile records from all sources to provide accurate and detailed information on all men in every North Carolina unit. Considering the volume of work, the editors did an outstanding job.

North Carolina Troops relies heavily on surviving muster and pay rolls located in the United States National Archives. The documents are available for all companies in 1861 and for most companies at various dates in 1862 through 1863.[2] For 1864, there are only records for 30 August, and there are none for 1865. To complicate matters, companies were not consistent in how records were kept. For example, on rolls dated late December 1862, Company I lists five men absent with leave and 35 AWOL while Company K lists 25 absent with leave and only three AWOL. One suspects that there was in reality little or no difference in why men from the two companies were not present.

I began by assembling a database of all men listed in *North*

Carolina Troops as serving in the 30th, omitting those who enlisted but never reported or who were dismissed as unfit for service in 1861. Some errors that crept into *North Carolina Troops* were corrected by reading all of the Individual Jackets or Personnel Folders of the 30th North Carolina found in the National Archives.[3] While the errors uncovered were not numerous, some were serious. Here are two examples.

Both *North Carolina Troops* and National Archives Jackets list one man as Private A. Fields, Company H and Private Absalom F. Fields, Company K. There are also documents in the Jackets that refer to a Private Anderson Fields. There was in reality only one man, a native of Pontotoc, Mississippi, a 32-year-old farm laborer who worked in 1860 for David Townsend, a wealthy man, originally from North Carolina. A.F. Fields joined Company H in September of 1863 and deserted on 20 November 1863. He appears next when captured in the Farmville, Virginia, hospital on 6 April 1865. He declared to his captors that he was a member of Company K. I have listed him with Company H.

John C. Williams of Company A is reported by *North Carolina Troops* to have died of typhoid in Wilmington, North Carolina, on 23 June 1863. The man who died was actually a "J.D. Williams" whose card was mistakenly placed in John C. Williams' Personal Jacket. Private John C. Williams in May 1863 was on detached duty in Virginia with battalion, or division, assigned to signal duty. In July 1863, he was assigned to the same duty in North Carolina under D.H. Hill. Returning to Virginia in 1864, he did signal work through 30 August 1864.

Reading the Personal Jackets provided much additional information on individuals not included in *North Carolina Troops.* All data found on furloughs, hospitalization, captures, wounds or AWOL/deserted as well as when and if a man returned, were added to the database.

For each month from September 1861 through April 1865, I recorded when men were killed or left the regiment for any reason. I then noted for the same month all men who joined or returned to the regiment for any reason. This gives a base number of men present at the beginning of each month.

Despite meticulous attention to detail, it must be said that the results should always be viewed as the upper limit of possibilities and treated as "no more than." The weakest point is accounting for men left behind sick or even sick in the hospital. It is likely that only a minority of such men appear anywhere in the records. Consider three examples. In the fall of 1861 and first half of 1862, Louis McLeod writes that very often dozens of men were so sick they could not train.[4] None of those he mentions appear in the records. On 24 July 1862, Colonel Parker wrote to his wife that the regiment had "more than 250 present sick, besides a good many in the Hospitals, in and around Richmond ... only about 300 present for duty."[5] The records show around 725 men present or accounted for. Just about the total Colonel Parker mentions if 150 to 175 were hospitalized and 250 present but sick.

In the summer of 1864, the regiment was with General Early moving to Washington. We have uncovered several members whose absences were not noted in *North Carolina Troops* or any official records. J.J. Goodin[6] wrote to his father that he and fellow Company D soldier William W. Cooper[7] and "several boys from the regiment" were in Winchester, Virginia. They had hoped to join up with the regiment but were now left behind and feared capture if they ventured beyond Winchester. They were, therefore, waiting for the unit's return.[8]

Goodin had enlisted in March 1864, and other letters to his parents written in May and June 1864 indicate that he was hospitalized with disease for much of that time. It is possible that he never joined the unit at all until the autumn of 1864 even though official records indicate that he was there from March on.

Another member of Company D, Francis Canady,[9] wrote that same month of July 1864 he had been in a hospital in Charlottesville for five weeks. He was sending the letter by John King[10] who had been furloughed.[11] Canaday's National Archives Personal Jacket does show him hospitalized but King does not appear in the records as furloughed until 15 September 1864; in October, he was hospitalized in Raleigh with a gunshot wound. In this one month, July 1864, there were unrecorded absences of a minimum of six to eight men, and probably more.

From September 1861 through April 1865, 1,506 men served in the 30th Regiment. The patriotic reaction to secession and invasion brought out large numbers of volunteers in 1861. By the end of that year, 944 men (62.9 percent of the total) had enlisted or been assigned to the 30th. The actual number present or accounted for by the spring of 1862 was 752.[12] Two hundred additional troops had been enrolled but not yet arrived at the regiment. In addition, the number hospitalized sick or sent home to recuperate at times numbered well over a hundred. The best estimate is that the roster reached around 800 men and officers in May 1862 and around 900 in June. There is every reason to believe that the number present was perhaps 100 less in each month due to disease, but that cannot be precisely determined.

When the regiment was preparing to leave for Richmond after 1 June, it was at its high strength for the war: 922 men and officers present or accounted for. The data show 111 men sick in a hospital or quarters at mid–May. We know from a letter of Louis H. McLeod that a large number were left behind when the regiment moved out and that a few of them joined the regiment in the second week of June in Virginia.[13] The last six months of 1862 would see the 30th involved in some of the bloodiest battles of the war, and numbers of men began to fall. This was due not only to death, wounds and capture but desertion or going AWOL. By December of 1862, the number of available men had dropped by about half to 499.

The 316 enlistments in 1862 (21 percent of the total) were largely the result of the draft put into place in the spring. The largest numbers joined in March—102—and September, after the harvest—67.

By September 1862, the Confederate Congress recognized that the first conscription law would not suffice. It, therefore, passed a second law.[14] One might expect that this second law would have eliminated some of the automatic exemptions to the draft but such was not the case. In fact, a few new exemptions were added, including for the first time membership in the Society of Friends.[15] The solution embraced was to extend the upper age for the draft from 35 to 45. As 1863 began, resistance to the draft in some parts of North Carolina grew to the point of armed resistance. In Yadkin County, some 20 to 30 conscripts seized a schoolhouse and fought off the local militia. Desperate measures and paying large bounties brought in 215 (14.3 percent of the total) troops in 1863.[16]

In early 1863, numbers present improved as men returned from sick or wounded furloughs, new recruits arrived and others came back after spending the winter AWOL. On 1 February, 651 men were present or accounted for. However, 1863 would see the 30th in heavy fighting at Chancellorsville, Gettysburg and a host of other smaller battles, one of which in November would prove to be the most disastrous day in the history of the regiment. By 1 May, attrition had reduced the 30th to 604; 506 crossed the Potomac in June, reached Carlisle, Pennsylvania, and then dropped back to Gettysburg. At the end of 1863, 570 men could be accounted for.

On 28 December 1863, changes were once again made in the conscription laws. This third draft law eliminated one of the features that to the modern mind seems extremely odious—the ability to hire a substitute. From that date on, no person could escape conscription by paying a substitute.

In 1864, Confederate Congress grew increasingly panicked about the lack of men to refill the depleted regiments.[17] On 5 January 1864, it was decreed that no one was exempt from service on the grounds of having paid a substitute. If there were no other reasons for exemption, such men were now liable to being drafted. There were already rumors circulating in camps about this in December 1863. Rufus D. Stallings expressed what was doubtless general satisfaction about the change in a letter, "I think that is a good thing.... If they do it I say good.... I want all them that is living at their ease & speculating on the soldier to have to come in & feale some of a soldiers fealings."[18]

In February 1864, the Confederate government suspended *habeas corpus* for the draft; all white males 17–50, without exemptions, were now subject to the draft; all men 18–45 currently enrolled were extended for the duration of the war. Congress then decreed that all persons who had been discharged previously for any reason, save disability, were now again required to serve. Many letters were written by men previously discharged insisting that they were crucial to the war effort as civilians and protesting this change.[19] Probably few of these men were re-enrolled in the army because by the time appeals were dealt with, it was 1865 and the entire Confederate government was collapsing. By the summer of 1864, the Confederate Congress began at last to eliminate many of the automatic exemptions and even to make free men of color liable for service.[20]

The pressure on counties to meet their draft quotas caused great trauma for many men. J.N. Ballenton, a cooper from New Hanover County who enlisted at Fort Holmes on 14 June 1863 (Company C), gave the following account to his captors in Washington, D.C.: "[He] was taken from his shop by a file of men without being allowed an opportunity of seeing his family. Never fired a gun in the rebellion and took the first opportunity of deserting and came into the Union Lines at Kelly's Ford [November 8, 1863]."[21] In 1864, only 33 recruits (2.2 percent of the total) could be found. Thirteen of the 33 were just turned 18 or still 17. The last enlistment was 1 October 1864. There would be no more.

The penultimate year of the war, 1864, began with 470 men and officers, dropped to 339 after the horrors of May and by Christmas could only count 273 men. When April 1865 began, the regiment served as the Army of Northern Virginia's rear guard fleeing west from Petersburg. It could count 243 men.[22] Twenty-one men returned to the unit in the first week of April. Of those 264, three died, 13 were furloughed for wounds, 62 were captured, 34 were unaccounted for and 153 were left to surrender with Lee at Appomattox Court House on 9 April 1865.

	JAN	FEB	MAR	APR	MAY	JUN	JUL	AUG	SEP	OCT	NOV	DEC
1861									544	909	913	910
1862	900	904	914	989	1002	1037	953	799	782	700	691	656
1863	688	704	693	675	670	553	594	575	615	697	699	525
1864	544	558	548	549	546	389	378	341	295	283	265	254
1865	251	248	236	226								

Figure 22. Present or Accounted For on the First Day of Each Month

Chapter Notes

Introduction

1. For the path taken to secession, see Hugh Lefler and Albert Newsome, *The History of a Southern State: North Carolina.* Chapel Hill: University of North Carolina Press, 1954, pp. 420–425.

2. Guion Griffis Johnson, *Ante-Bellum North Carolina A Social History.* Chapel Hill: University of North Carolina Press, 1937, pp. 468–470.

3. General information on Moore County is taken from Manly Wade Wellman, *The County of Moore 1847–1947.* Southern Pines, NC: Moore County Historical Association, 1962. See pp. 38–60 for Civil War Companies.

Chapter 1

1. William M. Swann was elected captain of the company on 15 August 1861 at the age of 22. He was defeated for reelection when the company was reorganized on 1 May 1862, and he left the army. Swann spent the rest of the war as an enrolling officer for the Confederacy. All biographical sketches on men of the 30th were assembled from data gathered from the National Archives.

2. Frederick J. Swann, William Swann's older brother, was one of the largest planters in Moore County. The 1850 census showed him owning 34 slaves. When the Western Railroad reached his plantation, he opened a store and a rail depot which became known as Swann Station. The 1860 census missed the Swanns.

3. This railroad eventually became part of the Atlantic Coast Line Company. In the late 20th century, the line was removed and little trace today remains of this vital transportation link. For information on the Western Railroad see "Western Railroad Company," *North Carolina Business History.* https://www.historync.org/railroad-WRR.htm.

4. As the war progressed and North Carolina and Virginia railroads suffered from lack of repair and supplies, travel actually became slower. In the spring of 1863, Lt. A.A. Jackson returned to the regiment after a sick furlough home. He wrote that to his great pleasure the trip was easier than expected. He took a stage coach in Moore County at 6 p.m. on Thursday and arrived in Raleigh at 9 the next morning. That night he boarded a train at 11 and arrived at Richmond only 19 hours later at 6 p.m. Saturday. The next morning he made it to Hamilton's Crossing where he met a wagoner in only four hours.

5. Detail on the roundabout trip to Raleigh is taken from letters of Louis McLeod.

6. Camp Mangum was the primary camp of instruction in North Carolina for state troops. Its commanders included future Lieutenant General Daniel H. Hill and future Major General Stephen D. Ramseur. Camp Mangum encompassed the grounds now occupied by the state fairgrounds, N.C. State University Faculty Club, School of Veterinary Science and the N.C. Museum of Art.

7. Louis H. McLeod (occasionally

spelled Lewis and always pronounced Lewis) lived in the Long Street section of Moore County (now Lee County), North Carolina. He was married with four children and in 1860 owned real estate valued at $3,000 and personal property valued at $5,000. Much of the latter was represented by three slaves. He mustered in as a corporal in August 1861 and, after the reorganization of the company in May 1862, was elected 2nd lieutenant. He was wounded at Malvern Hill on 1 July 1862 and while recuperating contracted typhoid fever for either the second or third time. He was sent home on disability leave and died at home on 19 March 1863 of dropsy. Unless otherwise noted all references to McLeod are from the extensive collection of letters to and from him copied by the author (see bibliography).

8. This company organized itself as a cavalry company and was initially assigned to the 20th N.C. Infantry. Somehow 11 companies had been placed in the 20th, and on 8 October 1861 it was reassigned and became the last company to join the 30th.

9. Camp Wyatt was south of Wilmington. It was used occasionally as a temporary base for units connected to Fort Fisher or other Wilmington defenses. It was named for Pvt. Henry L. Wyatt of the 1st North Carolina (Bethel) Regiment, believed to have been the first Confederate soldier killed in action.

10. Eliza McLeod wrote Louis on 1 December 1861 that she needed to go to Fayetteville for necessities. She was anxious about the trip because of her advanced pregnancy but felt she had no choice. Home was near the railroad so she could travel by train. She planned to sell "what otse we had lefte [after sowing] and too barles of flower to tri to get something to eat." On 8 December, she reported she had been to town and home safely. She received "fifty cents for otes six dolors and a half for flower and I paid eighteen cents for shuger and I bot fore pound of coffee and paid too dolors for it."

11. Alexander Duncan Moore was named captain of Company E, Wilmington Light Artillery in May of 1861. The company had no weapons until October when they were given six brass field pieces which they were showing off to the 30th Regiment. When North Carolina seceded, Moore was a cadet at West Point. He resigned and volunteered for North Carolina's troops. On 3 August 1863, he was named colonel of the 66th North Carolina Regiment. On 3 June 1864, he was wounded in the neck by a Union sharpshooter and quickly died.

12. Disease, swamps, bad water, insects and melancholy would plague not just the 30th but the entire army for most of the war. A superb discussion of health issues in 1862 can be found in Kathryn S. Meier, "No Place for the Sick: Nature's War on Civil War Soldier Mental and Physical Health in the 1862 Peninsula and Shenandoah Valley Campaigns," *Journal of the Civil War Era* 1, no. 2 (2011): pp. 176–206.

Chapter 2

1. Hal Bridges, *Lee's Maverick General: Daniel Harvey Hill.* Lincoln: University of Nebraska Press, 1991.

2. One man told his Union captors that he had been in the U.S. Artillery during the Mexican War but the claim cannot be verified.

3. Walter F. Draughan was a 40-year-old liquor merchant from Cumberland County. In 1860, he was married with one child and owned real estate valued at $7,000 and personal property, including nine slaves, valued at $23,000.

4. James T. Kell of Mecklenburg County was first elected captain of Company K, 30th North Carolina on 13 September 1861 and on 26 September 1861 elected major. He would resign from the army in August of 1863 because of disability from wounds. He was missed in the 1860 census.

5. Alexander D. Betts (1832–1918), graduate of University of North Carolina, was a Methodist minister when he became chaplain of the 30th North Carolina. It is apparent from Colonel Parker's letters to his wife in the winter of 1861

that he had a low opinion of the Reverend Mr. Betts' ability. Betts would seem, however, to have shared the dangers and the hardships with the men and did his best to comfort them. Around 1910, his diary, evidently edited by his son, was published as *Experience of a Confederate Chaplain.* Eastern Digital Resources (www. researchonline.net). Apparently the 58th North Carolina had no chaplain until May 1864. Michael G. Hardy, *The Fifty-eighth North Carolina Troops: Tar Heels in the Army of Tennessee.* Jefferson, NC: McFarland, 2010, p. 105. Hereinafter cited as Hardy, *Fifty-eighth.*

6. John Wesley Bone was 18 when he volunteered in September 1861, from Nash County. He would be among those surrendering at Appomattox Court House, Virginia, in April 1865. His memoir of the war, written many years later, has been well-edited by Julianne and David Mehegan and published as *Record of a Soldier in the Late War: The Confederate Memoir of John Wesley Bone.* Hingham, MA: Chinquapin Publishers, 2014. Hereinafter cited as Bone, *Record of a Soldier.*

7. Francis Marion Parker was born 21 September 1827 and grew up in Tarboro, North Carolina. His family was among the wealthy planters of eastern North Carolina. In the census of 1850, he is listed as owning 26 slaves. Though wounded grievously several times, he would survive the war. His numerous letters to his wife and others have been masterfully edited by Michael W. Taylor who added copious, very scholarly descriptions of Colonel Parker and the military activities of the 30th North Carolina. Michael W. Taylor, Ed. *To Drive the Enemy from Southern Soil: The Letters of Col. Francis Marion Parker and the History of the 30th Regiment North Carolina Troops.* Dayton, OH: Morningside House, 1998. Hereinafter cited as Parker, *Letters.*

8. Francis Parker (Camp Wyatt) to his wife Sarah Parker (Tarboro) 29 October 1861. Parker, *Letters,* p. 98.

9. John Witherspoon wrote that some men were being court-martialed for an attack on a colonel of another regiment. John Witherspoon (Camp Wyatt) to Hassie Witherspoon (Mecklenburg County, N.C.) 26 February 1862. Witherspoon's letters to his wife have been transcribed and privately published. Cited herein as Witherspoon Letters.

10. H. Taylor, Assistant Adjutant General (Richmond, Va.) to General French (Wilmington, N.C.) 23 April 1862. *Records of the War of the Rebellion,* S1, IX, XX, p. 453.

11. John B. Oates, *The Story of Fayetteville.* Fayetteville, NC: Dowd Press, Third Edition, 1981, pp 279–284.

12. For more detail on the mechanics of firing muskets in union and on duties of company officers and non-commissioned officers, refer to Hardy, *The Fifty-eighth,* pp. 31–32, 36. The 58th was raised in the mountains of western North Carolina and was different from the 30th in many ways. Unfortunately, Hardy gives very few indications of wealth and social status of the men of the 58th. However, he does an excellent job of detailing daily life and the military career of the 58th.

13. The full order of battle is unknown but William Ardrey in his diary noted on 26 May 1862 that Company H, under Captain Wicker, held the right flank of the regiment and Company D, under Captain Grisson, held the left flank. William E. Ardrey (1839–1907) in 1860 was a student at Davidson College. His father was a Mecklenburg County planter with real estate valued at $25,000 and personal property worth $42,000 including 47 slaves. He volunteered for the 1st N.C. Regiment in 1861 and became a private in Company K, 30th North Carolina on 10 February 1862. He was promoted to 2nd lieutenant on 1 May 1862, 1st lieutenant on 1 September 1863 and captain on 7 November 1863. He was furloughed from 3 June 1864 to 7 July 1864 resulting from a wound in the head. He was hospitalized for acute rheumatism in November 1862 and again in July 1863. He surrendered at Appomattox with the regiment. After the war he served several terms in the North Carolina House and North Carolina Senate. Ardrey kept a diary of his life with the 30th North Carolina. The original is

located in Davidson College Archives, Manuscript Number DC001, folders 3–11. Hereinafter cited as Ardrey, *Diary*.

14. John Witherspoon mentioned in a letter of 29 May 1862 that the drill was so hard that men occasionally fainted. In March 1863, he mentions that the regiment was drilling every day from 7–8 and from 11–12 in the morning and from 4–5 p.m. Witherspoon Letters.

Chapter 3

1. *Public Laws of the State of North Carolina Passed by the General Assembly, at Its Session of 1860-'61.* May be accessed at https://digital.ncdcr.gov/digital/collection/p249901coll22/id/178470.

2. Second Special Session of the General Assembly 1861. Chapter 17, Section 9. The act stated that these men or women could be free persons of color. No indication is given of rate of pay.

3. National Archives, Record Group 109, Compiled Military Service Records, North Carolina. In the 1920s, archivists filled out note cards on each Civil War soldier and placed the cards in personal jackets or folders, arranged by unit and alphabetical within units. In many cases, the jackets also include original documents relative to the soldier. Available on microfilm (North Carolina is M 270 (580 rolls)) or online through Ancestry.com and Fold3. National Archives Personal Jacket of John C. McMillan (Company E) and Personal Jacket of William E. Drake (Company B). Both are for the four days 7–10 September 1861. Hereinafter cited as National Archives, Personal Jacket.

4. The 30th North Carolina had at least five fully enrolled soldiers who were free mulattos.

5. In years past, many of the stories of black Confederates came from seeing these hired black civilians as soldiers.

6. Hardy Harris lived near Rollins Store, Moore County. He was a free mulatto, born in 1830. In 1860, he was married with one child. Next door to Harris lived Ingram Bass, also a free mulatto, born in 1835. Bass was married with no children in 1860. Each man had personal property of $25. They were both laborers on the railroad that was being extended from Rollins Store (Jonesboro) to the Egypt coal mine.

7. Louis McLeod (Camp Wyatt) to Eliza McLeod (Moore County, N.C.) 23 February 1862.

8. John G. Witherspoon was a 23-year-old farmer when he enrolled in Company K in September 1862 as first sergeant. In 1860, he was married with one child and real estate of $4,000 and personal property of $11,000, including six slaves. By 1862, his father had died and it is likely that he inherited a number of slaves. His letters and actions indicate a man of considerable wealth. He was, for example, able to secure two long furloughs of indulgence—unheard of for poor enlisted men—August 1862 and February 1863. In addition, he was twice sent home sick or for debility. With the reorganization of the company in May 1862, he was elected captain. He was killed at Kelly's Ford, Virginia, on 7 November 1863. His letters to his wife Hassie Witherspoon are available through the 30th North Carolina Reenactment Unit.

9. John Witherspoon (Culpepper Court House, Va.) to Hassie Witherspoon (Mecklenburg County, N.C.) 22 September 1862. Witherspoon Letters.

10. National Archives, Personal Jacket John C. McMillan.

11. Joseph Green was a 46-year-old wealthy farmer who raised up Company C as its captain in July 1861. In 1860, he was married with three children and owned real estate valued at $4,000 and personal property valued at $28,500, including 29 slaves. When Company C was reorganized in May 1862, Green was not reelected and he resigned from the army.

12. National Archives, Personal Jacket Joseph Green.

13. National Archives, Personal Jacket Buckner D. Williams.

14. This horse probably belonged to Buckner D. Williams. He was first elected 1st lieutenant of Company B, then assistant quartermaster of the regiment with the rank of captain on 26 September 1861.

In November 1863, he would be promoted to brigade quartermaster and leave the unit.

15. Abner Flynn Harrington, b. 30 June 1830, d. 27 March 1873. He enlisted as a private in Company H on 23 September 1861 and in the course of the war was promoted to first sergeant. He was among those who surrendered at Appomattox. In 1860, he was a farmer with $2,000 of real property and $5,000 of personal property. In addition, he owned three slaves.

16. James Knox Polk Harrington was the oldest son of A.F. Harrington's older brother John. In 1863, he turned 18 (b. 8 March 1845), went to Virginia and joined Company D, 3rd N.C. Cavalry—Highland Rangers. He was present or accounted for through October 1864. He survived the war and was called all his life "Poke."

17. A.F. Harrington (Camp Wyatt) to J.K.P. Harrington (Harnett County, N.C.) 23 April 1862. All references to A.F. Harrington unless otherwise noted are from letters in the possession of the author (see bibliography).

18. You get a good sense of what Wilmington became from Robert J. Cooke, *Wild, Wicked, Wartime Wilmington*. Wilmington, NC: Dram Tree Books, 2009.

19. Louis McLeod (Camp Lamb) to Eliza McLeod (Moore County, N.C.) 27 May 1862.

20. J.G. Witherspoon (Camp Wyatt) to Hassie Witherspoon (Mecklenburg County, N.C.) 17 November 1861. Witherspoon Letters.

21. Tandy Walker was Eliza McLeod's nephew. He volunteered on 15 August 1861, aged 24. He was present or accounted for through August 1864 when he seems to have gone AWOL. He was captured at Raleigh and paroled on 20 April 1865. He lived with his uncle John Walker in 1860 in the Rollins Store section of Moore County.

22. Hassie Witherspoon and the wife of another officer visited the camp early in March 1862.

23. Rufus D. Stallings was a 24-year-old overseer when he enrolled in Company F as a private in May 1862. He was unmarried and in 1860 owned no real estate and personal property of $75. He was one of the fortunate few in the 30th. He was never wounded, never captured, never officially admitted to a hospital and surrendered with the unit at Appomattox.

24. Rufus D. Stallings (Virginia) to Elizabeth Ward (Rocky Mount) [first page missing so no date available]. Rufus Delano Stallings letters, East Carolina University Archives. https://digital.lib.ecu.edu/3340. After the war, Stallings and Ward married.

25. Amusements and sports were commonplace during time away from battle. Baseball, snowball fights, rabbit chasing, wrestling, races, boxing and fishing often took place. For much more detail about sports and amusements in both armies, see Lawrence W. Fielding, "War and Trifles: Sport in the Shadows of Civil War Army Life," *Journal of Sport History* 4, no. 2 (1977): pp. 151–68. www.jstor.org/stable/43609251.

26. James Deaton was a 24-year-old well-digger living in Chatham County when he enrolled as a private in Company H in August 1861. He was married with no children in 1860, owned no real estate but $50 of personal property. He was promoted to sergeant in May 1862. He was wounded at Gaines Mill and from late 1864 until the end of the war was away from the regiment on detached service.

27. Louis McLeod (Camp Wyatt) to Eliza McLeod (Moore County, N.C.) 20 November 1861.

28. Francis M. Moore was elected 2nd lieutenant of the company on 15 August 1861 at the age of 21. He was residing in Moore County but his father, James Moore, was a large planter in Brunswick near Wilmington. The senior Moore owned real property valued at $13,000 and personal property valued at $45,675. In addition, the plantation housed 39 male slaves and 17 female slaves.

29. Louis McLeod (near Wilmington) to Eliza McLeod (Moore County, N.C.) 8 October 1861.

30. Francis Moore (New Brunswick County, N.C.) to William Swann (Camp Wyatt) 13 February 1862. National

Archives, Personal Jacket Francis M. Moore.

31. David P. Morris enlisted on 15 August 1861, aged 42. He was a cousin of Eliza Walker McLeod whose mother was Mary "Polly" Morris. Morris was wounded and captured at Gettysburg, paroled and returned to duty late in 1864. In April 1865, he was again captured at High Bridge, Virginia, and confined at Point Lookout, Maryland, where he died on 3 May 1865 of "chronic diarrhea." He is missing from the 1860 census. In 1850, he was a farmer living in a large household headed by David Gaster.

32. John Walker was Eliza McLeod's brother. He lived in the nearby Rollins Store section of Moore County, was a farmer with $500 real property and $1,500 personal property. He enlisted in Company I, Second Regiment of N.C. Cavalry (19th Regiment of NCT) on 13 July 1861, aged 35. He was elected sergeant. On 28 May 1862, he was discharged as a result of the "conscript act," probably because he was overaged.

33. Abel Douglas was a close friend and perhaps relative who lived nearby in Harnett County, N.C. He was born in 1818. In 1860, he was married with seven children. He owned $2,000 real property and $7,000 personal property in 1860.

34. This behavior was nothing compared to that of many Louisiana soldiers. Terry L. Jones, "Wharf-Rats, Cutthroats and Thieves: The Louisiana Tigers, 1861–1862," *Louisiana History: The Journal of the Louisiana Historical Association* 27, no. 2 (1986): pp. 147–65. www.jstor.org/stable/4232496.

35. James Mashburn lived in Moore County and enlisted on 15 August 1861 at the age of 30. He was wounded at Malvern Hill, Virginia, 1 July 1862 and died 3 July 1862.

36. Louis McLeod (Camp Wyatt) to Eliza McLeod (Moore County, N.C.) 8 January 1862.

37. William W. Sillers in 1860 was a lawyer who owned a large plantation in Sampson County valued at $10,000 with 50 slaves. He graduated with third honors from the University of North Carolina

in 1859. He was unmarried and lived with his sister Frances and brother-in-law Doctor Almond Holmes. He mustered in Sampson Rangers on 20 April 1861 at the age of 22. He was elected 1st lieutenant of the company on 3 August 1861, promoted to major on 1 May 1862 and transferred to the Field and Staff of the 30th North Carolina. On 3 September 1863, he was promoted to lieutenant colonel of the regiment and commanded the regiment in the absence of Colonel Parker. He was wounded at Malvern Hill and killed at Kelly's Ford on 9 November 1863. Fourteen letters written by Sillers and one letter describing his death have survived and are housed in the Rare Book Division of the University of Notre Dame. The letters are available online at http://www.rarebooks.nd.edu/digital/civil_war/letters/sillers-holmes/. Cited herein as Sillers Letters.

38. William Sillers (Virginia) to his sister (Clinton, N.C.) 9 February 1863. Sillers Letters.

39. Tobacco was not yet a ubiquitous cash crop in North Carolina. It is clear from Eliza McLeod's letters to Louis that they grew none at all.

40. Andrew Brown, Jr., was born on Christmas Day, 1803. His mother was Nancy Hinton and sister to McLeod's mother. In 1860, he was a farmer with $7,500 of real property and $26,100 of personal property, by local terms a wealthy man.

Chapter 4

1. French ended the war with the rank of major general and fought in Virginia and as a division commander in the Army of Tennessee. At the end of the war, he was under Joseph Johnston in the delaying action leading to the fall of Atlanta. The general wrote an extensive autobiography. *Two Wars: An Autobiography of General Samuel B. French.* Nashville: Confederate Veteran, 1910. Also available online at https://archive.org/details/twowarsanautobio00fren.

2. Francis Parker (Wilmington) to

his wife (Tarboro, N.C.) 27 March 1862. Parker, *Letters*, pp. 149–150.

3. Some officers seem to have had a great deal of "superfluous baggage." John G. Witherspoon was in a tent with a wood floor and had a nice chair and a bed stead. John Witherspoon (Camp Wyatt) to Hassie Witherspoon (Mecklenburg County, N.C.) 10 November 1861. Witherspoon Letters.

4. A.F. Harrington (Jacksonville, N.C.) to John Harrington (Harnett County, N.C.) *circa* 22 April 1862.

5. In 1860, there were several women and married couples named Sanders in Onslow County. It is not possible to know which one was Mrs. Sanders.

6. A.F. Harrington (Jacksonville, N.C.) to John Harrington (Harnett County, N.C.) *circa* 22 April 1862.

7. Cornelius Patrick was a native of Putnam County, NY. He mustered in a private and was elected 2nd lieutenant in August 1861. He was a merchant in Sampson County but not found in the 1860 census. From 1 December 1861 through the end of February 1862, he was mostly home on sick furlough.

8. James C. Holmes in 1860 was a merchant living in Sampson County owning real estate worth $2,600 and personal property valued at $18,750. He was married with no children. On 20 April 1861, he was elected 2nd lieutenant when the Sampson Rangers were organized. In August 1861 when the captain of the company left to be lieutenant colonel in the 20th Regiment NCT, Holmes was promoted to captain. In September 1863, he was promoted to major and transferred to the Field and Staff of 30th North Carolina. On 19 August 1864, he was declared unfit for duty due to partial paralysis on the left side, chronic diarrhea and general debility. He was retired to the Invalid Corps. It is unclear what caused his disability. There are no records of wounds or hospitalization.

9. James C. Holmes (Wilmington) to the Secretary of War (Richmond) *circa* 8 May 1862. National Archives, Personal Jacket James C. Holmes.

10. General French (Wilmington) to

Secretary of War (Richmond) 9 May 1862. National Archives, Personal Jacket James C. Holmes.

11. Francis Parker (Camp Wyatt) to Sarah Parker (Tarboro) 6 December 1861. Parker, *Letters*, p. 114.

12. This was probably Andrew Brown, Jr., who speculated in chickens. There was, however, a younger Andrew Brown in Company H. He was a laborer and apparently unrelated to the wealthier Browns.

13. The head of the family was Jesse B. Goodin married to Frances Brassfield. In 1860, the household was composed of ten persons and reported personal property of $575. The exact relationship with Wesley Brassfield is unclear but in letters he refers to Jesse and Frances Goodin as his parents. Duke University, Perkins Library, Special Collections. Goodin, Jesse B. DO3570923T. Thirty-eight letters mostly from J.W. Brassfield, John C. Goodin and Joseph Goodin to members of the Goodin Family. Cited herein as Goodin Letters.

14. William Sillers (Virginia) to his sister (Clinton, N.C.) 16 February 1862. Sillers Letters.

15. Eliza McLeod (Moore County, North Carolina) to Louis McLeod (Near Wilmington, North Carolina) 25 February 1862.

16. Hill's opinions are summarized in Hal Bridges, *Lee's Maverick General: Daniel Harvey Hill*. Lincoln: University of Nebraska Press, 1991.

17. John C. McMillan cannot be found in the 1860 census report, but in 1850 he was a student living on his father's large farm valued at $6,000. At the age of 23, he joined the Duplin Turpentine Boys in August 1861 and was elected captain. In the fall of 1862, he apparently left his company for a time without permission and was publicly reprimanded for so doing. He was wounded in the wrist and hip at Chancellorsville on 3 May 1863; wounded again in May 1864; wounded in the right side on 6 April 1865. He was with the company on 8 April 1865 at Appomattox Court House.

18. Willis Goodin (Camp Wyatt) to John Goodin (at home on sick leave) 23

February 1862. Goodin Letters. He wrote that none of the Nurse Rivers Guards had signed up. It was too early to decide.

19. John Witherspoon (Camp Holmes) to Hassie Witherspoon (Mecklenburg County, N.C.) 5 April 1862. Witherspoon Letters.

20. Benjamin Morrow was 28 when he enrolled in Company K in September 1861. He is not found in the 1860 census but in 1850 was a student living with his father who owned $7,200 of real estate. He resigned from the company when he was not reelected captain.

21. Memory F. Mitchell, *Legal Aspects of Conscription and Exemption in North Carolina 1861–1865*. Chapel Hill: University of North Carolina Press, 1965, pp. 13ff.

22. Jennifer Van Zant, "Confederate Conscription and the North Carolina Supreme Court," *The North Carolina Historical Review* 72, no. 1 (1995): pp. 54–75. www.jstor.org/stable/23521870. Richmond Mumford Person, chief justice of the North Carolina Supreme Court, often ruled in favor of plaintiffs and against the conscription acts. The Court never ruled that the Confederate Conscription Acts were constitutional but court rulings assumed they were. Van Zant notes that in the absence of a comprehensive Confederate court system—authorized by the Confederate constitution but never fully created—the state court ruled on national laws.

23. This exemption, so disturbing today, caused little complaint in 1862. Even poor men no doubt believed that slaves/blacks had to be kept under control. It was also just one more law in favor of the rich, no worse than others. There are no complaints about the exemption in the letters written by men of the 30th. Aaron Sheehan-Dean notes that he found not a single comment on the exemption in Virginia soldiers' letters. Aaron Sheehan-Dean, *Why Confederates Fought: Family & Nation in Civil War Virginia*. Chapel Hill: University of North Carolina Press, 2007, p. 103. Hereinafter cited as Sheehan-Dean, *Confederates*.

24. James Stephens Harrington, the oldest of ten siblings, was born 1807, died 1888. In 1860, he was married with five children at home or in school. His farm was valued at $2,250 and his personal property at $15,000. He was a member of the North Carolina House of Commons from 1858–1861. After the war he secured a pardon, joined the Republican Party and was a member of the Reconstructionist State Senate in 1868–1869.

25. In Virginia, the fee paid a substitute in the summer of 1862 apparently reached the astronomical amount of $1,000. Just before the practice was ended, some paid as much as $2,000. Sheehan-Dean, *Confederates*, pp. 96–97, 143.

26. James Oscar Abner Kelly was born 28 July 1833. He served as captain of his company until the war ended. He was a cousin of Eliza Walker McLeod.

27. Eliza McLeod (Moore County, N.C.) to Louis McLeod (near Wilmington) 25 February 1862.

28. E.J. [Elizabeth Jane] Berreman (Moore County, N.C.) to Louis McLeod (near Wilmington) 3 March 1862. Berreman wrote that Fred Swann, Captain William Swann's brother, was drafted but hired Scarborough for $75 as his substitute. She mentions other wealthy locals who were searching for substitutes. One man was drafted and left at once for Raleigh with a local politician to try and get free. He was reported to have said "he would not care if his horses would runaway & kill him on his way from Carthage."

29. Reorganizations took place in a great many regiments and in some cases many officers were voted out. Hale notes that in the 3rd Texas Cavalry all company commanders and most of the lieutenants were changed. As a result of resignations after the reorganization, 208 men resigned and left the unit. The new officers were younger and richer than the original ones. Douglas Hale, "The Third Texas Cavalry: A Socioeconomic Profile of a Confederate Regiment," *Military History of the Southwest* 19 (Spring 1989): p. 24. In the 58th North Carolina, not only did officers who were not confirmed resign, a good number of those who were

reelected also left. Most of them were over 45 years old and had found military life much too difficult. Hardy, *Fifty-eighth,* p. 51.

30. Sheehan-Dean, *Confederates,* p. 67, reports that this happened in many Virginia companies and for the same reason: company officers going home in the spring of 1862 rather than suffering the hardships of camp with their soldiers.

31. Jesse J. Wicker in 1860 was an unmarried man living on his father's modest farm valued at $3,000 in Moore County. His father had personal property valued at $1,000, doubtless the one slave he owned. Jesse Wicker joined his company in August 1861 as a sergeant, became 2nd lieutenant in February 1862, and when the company was reorganized in May 1862, he was elected captain. He was wounded during the invasion into Maryland in September 1862, only returning to active duty in January 1863. On 12 May 1864, he was captured and was still a prisoner of war when the war ended in 1865. When he took the oath of loyalty in June 1865, he was described as 6 feet tall, of ruddy complexion, brown hair and grey eyes.

32. Archibald McIntosh cannot be located in the 1860 census, but in 1850 he and his brother Daniel were children on their father's small farm valued at only $53. For most of December 1861, Archibald McIntosh was furloughed home sick.

33. Daniel McIntosh was away from the company from mid-November 1861 through April 1862 listed sick at home. This may be why he was not reelected lieutenant.

34. Henry J. McNeill cannot be located in the 1860 census. In 1850, he was a child in his father's household in Moore County. The father owned no property of any kind, called himself a "farmer." McNeill was mustered in as a corporal and elected 1st lieutenant on 1 May 1862. He was slightly wounded at Gettysburg but missed no duty as a result. Again wounded near Spotsylvania Court House on 19 May 1864, he was absent wounded until early March 1865 when he resigned

from the service, probably on grounds of disability.

35. Archibald A. Jackson was a turpentine distiller living in Moore County. He mustered in as a corporal in August 1861. He was unmarried and owned real estate valued at $502 and personal property valued at $500. During the war, he was hospitalized for both typhoid and small pox. He died on 12 May 1864 of wounds received at Spotsylvania Court House, Virginia. His letters home are preserved in the rare book section of University of Notre Dame Library. Jackson Family Correspondence, MSN/CW 5067: Rare Books and Special Collections, Hesburgh Libraries of Notre Dame. Hereinafter cited as Jackson Letters.

36. Louis McLeod (Camp Wyatt) to Eliza McLeod (Moore County, N.C.) 30 March 1862.

37. Buckner Williams enlisted in Company B at the age of 28 and in August 1861 was elected 1st lieutenant. He was named acting quartermaster on 26 September 1861 and promoted to captain. On 1 November 1861, he was officially named quartermaster. In the fall of 1863, he was promoted to major and brigade quartermaster and left the 30th. In 1860, he was a merchant in Warren County, married with one child; he owned real estate valued at $3,000 and personal property worth $17,850, including three slaves.

38. Unless otherwise stated all information in this section is from National Archives, Personal Jacket Buckner Williams.

39. Louis McLeod (eastern N.C.) to Eliza McLeod (Moore County, N.C.) 27 May 1862.

Chapter 5

1. Richard Bardolph in "Inconstant Rebels: Desertion of North Carolina Troops in the Civil War," *The North Carolina Historical Review* 41, no. 2 (1964) cites many letters and historians who blamed desertion on anger in the ranks over perceived inequity. Very interesting is a letter from D.H. Hill to Governor

Notes—Chapter 5

Zebulon B. Vance dated 26 April 1863. Hill rails against "...the capitalist, the extortioner...." Above all, he blames the exempt. Those men, getting rich off the war, Hill considered far worse than deserters.

2. Joseph T. Glatthaar, *Soldiering in the Army of Northern Virginia: A Statistical Portrait of the Troops Who Served Under Robert E. Lee.* Chapel Hill: University of North Carolina Press, 2011, pp. 9–10. Hereinafter cited as Glatthaar, *Soldiering.*

3. Aaron Sheehan-Dean, *Why Confederates Fought: Family & Nation in Civil War Virginia.* Chapel Hill: University of North Carolina Press, 2007.

4. Colin Edward Woodward, *Marching Masters: Slavery, Race, and the Confederate Army During the Civil War.* Charlottesville: University of Virginia Press. pp. 31ff. Hereinafter cited as Woodward, *Marching Masters.*

5. Keri Leigh Merritt, *Masterless Men: Poor Whites and Slavery in the Antebellum South.* Cambridge, UK: Cambridge University Press, 2017, pp. 286–322. This study insists that very large numbers of poor whites were opposed to the war, were forced into service and deserted in large numbers, while larger numbers of rich evaded the war. Hereinafter cited as Merritt, *Masterless Men.*

6. The Swann family is included in the 1870 census.

7. Merritt, *Masterless Men*, pp. 342ff.

8. The 1850 census estimates value of real estate but not personal property.

9. Glatthaar, *Soldiering.*

10. Merritt, *Masterless Men*, p. 16.

11. This is one area in which North Carolina was only next to lowest. Maryland only paid on average $9.71.

12. Glatthaar, *Soldiering*, p. 25, Figure 2.4.

13. Two apprentices; two blacksmiths; one cabinet maker; 21 carpenters; one clock repairer; 16 coopers; two distillers; three distillers of turpentine; three ditchers; two engineers; nine mechanics; six millers; one miller at gold mine; four painters; one plow maker; one seaman; one sieve maker; seven shoemakers; one textile worker; one stone mason; one sawmill superintendent; one tobacconist; one weaver; one well digger; three wheelwrights; one tanner; one miner.

14. Glatthaar, *Soldiering*, p. 24, Figure 2.4.

15. Wellman, *County of Moore*, volume II, p. 34ff.

16. There are exactly one dozen men who were students with a large degree of wealth among this number. It is quite possible that they were slave owners but not reflected by the census. Even if they are removed, well over 80 percent owned no slaves.

17. Patrick Doyle offers a good summary of the substitute system from its beginnings in the Revolution to its elimination by the Confederacy. He believes substitutes were eliminated not only for practical reasons of no longer serving the Confederate military, but because substitutes no longer met the evolving notions about manhood and duty. Patrick J. Doyle, "Replacement Rebels: Confederate Substitution and the Issue of Citizenship," *Journal of the Civil War Era* 8, no. 1 (2018): pp. 3–31.

18. Archibald Jackson wrote home criticizing a man who hired a substitute. Eliza McLeod more than once urged Louis to pay someone so he could come home.

19. The 55th North Carolina could count at least 64 substitutes. That regiment was formed late and, in the opinion of Jeffrey Girvan, most of the members were conscripted and had little loyalty to the Confederacy. Girvan, *The 55th North Carolina*, pp. 2, 5.

20. In October 1864, Virginia ended all exemptions and drafted 4,500 men. Sheehan-Dean, *Confederates*, p. 177.

21. Noe found newspaper advertisements late in 1863 offering $10,000 or considerable land for a substitute. This number is misleading because of the increasingly weak value of Confederate money. Kenneth W. Noe, "Alabama We Will Fight for Thee: the Initial Motivations of Later-enlisting Confederates," *Alabama Review* 62, no. 3 (July 2009): p. 182.

22. William Bass evidently made such a bargain with Lawrence Battle. Bass died of pneumonia in March 1863. Battle wrote asking for Bass's possessions ($4.50 and one knapsack with some clothing) to be sent to him. He asked for this as he was responsible for the five little children Bass left in his care. National Archives, Personal Jacket William Bass.

23. There was, in addition to three members of the Wake County Goodin family in Company D, the older half-brother Wesley Brassfield.

24. James Morgan was 22, enlisted in Company F August 1861. He was wounded at Malvern Hill, returned to duty December 1862, captured at Kelly's Ford 7 November 1863, exchanged 24 February 1865; no records after March 1865.

25. Thomas Morgan, the youngest of the Morgan brothers, was 17 when he volunteered in February 1864. He was wounded at Snickers Gap 18 July 1864 and hospitalized until March 1865 when he was furloughed home.

26. William Morgan was 20, enlisted in Company F August 1861. He was wounded in the invasion of Maryland in September 1862 and returned to duty in December 1862. He was admitted to Chimborazo in April 1863 suffering from pneumonia and returned to duty in June. In February 1864, he was admitted to Richmond Hospital #9 with an unnamed malady. He was present at the surrender at Appomattox Court House on 9 April 1865.

27. Duncan Goins was working as a farm laborer, aged 24 when he enlisted in Company H in August 1861. His father was a free mulatto carpenter with personal property of $150 who lived in Chatham County. He was admitted to Wilmington Hospital 8 March 1862 suffering with typhoid fever, from which he died on 10 March 1862.

28. Edward Goins was 21 years old when he volunteered for Company H on 15 August 1861. He was remarkable in that his records show no desertions, no times AWOL and no hospitalization. He surrendered with the regiment at Appomattox Court House.

29. Kevin Levin, *Searching for Black Confederates: The Civil War's Most Persistent Myth*. Chapel Hill: University of North Carolina Press, 2019. Mr. Levin was interviewed in Slate on the subject as well. Rebecca Onion, "Dismantling the Myth of the 'Black Confederate,'" Slate, 30 August 2019. https://slate.com/human-interest/2019/08/black-confederate-myth-history-book.amp.

30. In 1850, Chatham County, Pittsboro PO, line 37, dwelling 1231, family 1232. In 1860, Pittsboro PO, dwelling 333, family 307.

31. See census records for Edgecombe County, North Carolina. Tarboro PO, dwelling 1246, family 1165.

32. Merritt, *Masterless Men*, pp. 126ff.

33. Johnson, *Ante-Bellum NC*, p. 30.

34. Walter S. Turner was a 13-year-old clerk or student living in Nash County when he enlisted in Company I on 10 September 1861. His father owned personal property valued at $500. He was ranked as a musician. Turner spent December 1861 and much of January 1862 at home sick. He was discharged on 29 September 1862 as being underage according to the Conscription Act.

35. Thomas G. Smith was a farm laborer, aged 27, resident of Wake County when he enlisted in Company D on 10 August 1861. In 1860, he was married with three children and owned personal property valued at $75. He was hospitalized on 13 September 1862, diagnosed with *rheumatismas acutus*. On 2 October, he was sick furloughed. From 22 October 1862 through 10 March 1863, he was listed AWOL. From 10 April 1863 until 10 May 1863, he was hospitalized with typhoid fever. On 7 November 1863, he was among the large number captured at Kelly's Ford, Virginia, and he finished the war as a POW, being released on 19 June 1865.

36. James J. Loughlin (or Laughlin), born in Manchester, England, was residing in Norfolk, Virginia in 1860. He apparently lived with an older brother who was a shoemaker. When the war began, he was in Warren County, North Carolina, 21 years old; he enlisted in Company B on

16 August 1861. He mustered in as a sergeant but was quickly elected 3rd lieutenant. He was captured at Malvern Hill on 1 July 1862 and exchanged on 16 July 1862. He was again captured during the retreat from Gettysburg on 23 July 1863 and sent to the POW camp for officers at Johnson Island, Ohio. Some efforts may have been made to have the British ambassador to Washington, Lord Richard Lyons, intervene for his release but if so, they failed. (James J. Laughlin (Johnson Island, Ohio) to his father (unknown) 7 September 1864. National Archives, Personal Jacket James J. Loughlin). He was released on 11 June 1865.

37. Private Marlow joined the regiment at Richmond, Virginia, on 5 August 1862; he was a native of Edgecombe County. He was not found in the 1860 census, but in 1850 he was a cooper, head of household, married with five children. He had no property. On 29 January 1863, Marlow was admitted to Chimborazo Hospital Number 3 with pneumonia. He died on 5 February 1863 in the hospital.

38. Private Morris lived in Wake County where he was a miller when he enlisted in Company D, aged 40, on 10 August 1861. On 12 November 1862, he was admitted to Chimborazo Hospital diagnosed with typhoid-pneumonia; 14 November 1862 he was transferred to Petersburg Hospital suffering from acute dysentery. He died in Petersburg Hospital on 2 January 1863 attributed to typhoid fever.

39. Glatthaar, *Soldiering*, p. 23.

Chapter 6

1. Bell Irvin Wiley, *The Life of Johnny Reb: The Common Soldiers of the Confederacy*. Indianapolis: Bobbs-Merrill, 1943.

2. James M. McPherson, *For Cause & Comrades: Why Men Fought in the Civil War*. New York: Oxford University Press, 1997.

3. *Ibid.* p. 5.

4. Woodward, *Marching Masters*, p. 13.

5. *Ibid.* p. 39.

6. Sheehan-Dean, *Confederates*, p. 60.

7. Eliza McLeod (Moore County, N.C.) to Louis McLeod (Camp near Wilmington) 9 February 1862.

8. Louis McLeod (Camp Lamb) to Eliza McLeod (Moore County, N.C.) 15 June 1862.

9. Kenneth W. Noe, *Reluctant Rebels: The Confederates Who Joined the Army after 1861*. Chapel Hill: University of North Carolina Press, 2010, pp. 103–124.

10. William Marvel, *Lincoln's Mercenaries: Economic Motivation Among Union Soldiers During the Civil War*. Baton Rouge: Louisiana State University Press, 2018.

11. Kenneth Noe provides a succinct account of historians who held this view and how it has evolved. Kenneth W. Noe, "Alabama, We Will Fight for Thee," *Alabama Review* 62, no. 3 (July 2009): pp. 165–167.

12. "Run you damn rebels," is what Eliza McLeod heard the Union soldiers had said as they pursued fleeing North Carolinians on Roanoke Island.

13. The version by A.F. Harrington quoted above.

14. James L. Green (Camp Mangum) to Mary Green (Cleveland County, N.C.) 15 May 1863 [miss-labeled 1862]. Green Letters.

15. Louis McLeod (Near Richmond Virginia) to Eliza McLeod (Moore County, N.C.) 22 June 1862.

16. William Williamson was 16 when he enrolled in September 1861. He was a student, son of a well-to-do farmer in 1860. He was hospitalized for an unrecorded malady in December 1862 and subsequently discharged as being under-aged.

17. Aaron L. DeArmond was a 35-year-old farmer when he enlisted as sergeant in September 1861. In 1860, he owned real property worth $1,000 and personal property of $1,500. He was married with two children. He was held prisoner only four days after Antietam and was captured a second time at Kelly's Ford in November 1863, being exchanged on 10 June 1864. He was wounded 18 July 1864 and died of the wounds a month

later on 19 August. His letters seem to have been privately published by a member of the family in the late 20th century but could not be located for this study.

18. Moses Bently was the son of a carpenter who was 19 when he enlisted in September 1861. He was held for one week as a POW after Antietam; was wounded at Malvern Hill and again in August 1864. He was one of the many who went over to the Union Army in early April 1865 and was released in June 1865.

19. Ardrey, *Diary*, 3 and 4 October 1862.

20. Not all men who entered the army after 1861 were conscripts. Some, like those Louis McLeod recruited, were volunteers. Kenneth Noe, in his study of a sample of these men from different parts of the South, writes that they seem to have been motivated by support of slavery, a need to protect their state and the South from vile Yankee invaders and, very often, by the bounty. Poor men needed the money. Noe, *Motivations*, p. 180.

21. *North Carolina Troops*, p. 364; National Archives, Personal Jacket John W. Bray.

22. National Archives, Personal Jacket H.G. Rose.

23. National Archives, Personal Jackets Ralph Currin and William Currin.

24. National Archives, Personal Jacket John L. Miller.

25. *North Carolina Troops*, p. 392; National Archives, Personal Jacket Alfred Black.

26. Information taken from Manly Wade Wellman, *The County of Moore*, Vol II, pp. 34ff.

27. J.G. Witherspoon (Camp Wyatt) to Hassie Witherspoon (Cabarrus County, N.C.) 15 November 1861. Witherspoon Letters.

28. J.G. Witherspoon (Hamilton Crossing, Virginia) to Hassie Witherspoon (Cabarrus County, N.C.) 14 March 1863. Witherspoon Letters.

29. It is possible that the names are not properly assigned. The 1860 Census Slave Schedule lists three slaves on the McLeod Farm, one male 58, one female 40 and one male 10. In 1870 according to the

census, Henry McLeod, a man of color living in the same neighborhood as Eliza McLeod, said he was 53 and a woman Nellie, living with him, was 35. Arry is not there but five children aged from 17 to 4 are present. In some of Eliza McLeod's letters Nellee is referred to as "he," but her writing was very poor grammatically.

30. Eliza McLeod (Moore County, N.C.) to Louis McLeod (Camp Wyatt) 24 November 1861. This is one of the confusing references. Was Nellie plowing and working in the fields? Perhaps, but the pronoun is "he."

31. Eliza McLeod (Moore County, N.C.) to Louis McLeod (Camp Wyatt) 9 February 1862.

32. Louis McLeod (Wilmington, N.C.) to Eliza McLeod (Moore County, N.C.) 26 May 1862.

33. Eliza McLeod (Moore County, N.C.) to Louis McLeod (Camp Wyatt) 25 February 1862.

34. J.K.P. Harrington (Virginia) to Mary Elizabeth Harrington (Harnett County, N.C.) 17 August 1864.

35. Ardrey, *Diary*, 8 August 1863.

36. W.W. Sillers (Virginia) to his sister (North Carolina) 7 August 1863. Sillers Letters.

37. *Ibid.*

38. G.F. Williams (Virginia) to Dr. Holmes (North Carolina) 11 November 1863. Sillers Letters.

39. Francis Parker (Wilmington, N.C.) to his wife (Tarboro, N.C.) 14 February 1862. Parker, *Letters*, p. 129.

40. Henry Phillips was listed in the 1860 census as a free mulatto, 20 years old, who lived in the household of a prosperous white farmer.

41. Ardrey, *Diary*, 6 January 1864.

42. Hicks was described in the 1860 census as a mulatto farmer with $200 of real property and $200 of personal property. He had been born in Virginia, was 46 years old, married with seven children.

43. Francis Parker (Virginia) to Sarah Parker (Halifax County, N.C.) 26 January 1864. Parker, *Letters*, p. 311.

44. William Sillers (Camp near Fredericksburg, Va.) to his sister (North Carolina) 22 March 1863. Sillers Letters.

45. Francis Parker (Camp Wyatt) to Sarah Parker (Tarboro, N.C.) 14 November 1861. Parker, *Letters*, pp. 107–112.

46. Francis Parker (Camp Lamb) to Sarah Parker (Tarboro, N.C.) 23 March 1862. Parker, *Letters*, pp. 148–149.

47. For a discussion of chaplains and general organization of religion in the Army of Northern Virginia, see John Shepard, Jr., "Religion in the Army of Northern Virginia," *The North Carolina Historical Review* 25, No. 3 (July 1948): pp. 341–376. The author heaps praise on those who encouraged the practice of religion in the army. His own evident fervent belief distorts some of his analysis, but he does give a coherent outline of the development of the chaplain corps and the recruitment of the men.

48. A.F. Harrington (Orange Court House, Va.) to John Harrington (Harnett County, N.C.) 11 September 1863.

49. *Ibid.*

50. Revivalism was widespread in Virginia units as well. Sheehan-Dean, *Confederates*, pp. 131–132.

51. Ardrey, *Diary*, May 1863.

52. Rufus Stallings (Camp near Martinsburg, Va.) to Elizabeth Ward (Rocky Mount) 17 July 1863. Stallings Letters.

53. William Sillers (Near Orange Court House, Va.) to his sister (North Carolina) 22 August 1863. Sillers Letters.

54. A.F. Harrington (Orange Court House, Va.) to John Harrington (Harnett County, N.C.). 11 September 1863.

55. Ardrey, *Diary*, 2 September 1863.

56. Bone, *Record of a Soldier*, p. 67.

Chapter 7

1. Louis McLeod (two miles east of Richmond) to Eliza McLeod (Moore County, N.C.) 22 June 1862.

2. *Ibid.*

3. For an understanding of the military campaign, see Stephen W. Sears, *To the Gates of Richmond: The Peninsula Campaign*, New York, 1992, p. 256. Sears states that McClellan had around 99,000 combatants in the field and the largest

number Lee ever placed in the field was no more than 4/5 of Union forces.

4. Louis McLeod (Camp Holmes) to Eliza McLeod (Moore County, N.C.) 22 June 1862.

5. *Ibid.*

6. Denis Carr was a native of Ireland and volunteered in August 1861, was wounded at Gaines Mill and returned to duty about 14 July 1862. From 14 July through mid-August he was hospitalized sick. He was discharged on 22 September 1862 under provisions of the Conscription Act as "being an alien." In 1860, he was a laborer on the Western Railroad being built across Moore County, N.C.

7. Louis McLeod (near Richmond, Va.) to Eliza McLeod (Moore County, N.C.) 22 June 1862.

8. One of those wounded was Louis McLeod who we have referred to so often in these pages. He was hospitalized in Richmond and while recovering from his wound contracted once again typhoid fever. He was furloughed home and never recovered. He died of dropsy (heart failure) in the spring of 1863.

9. To see the invasion and the threat to the capital Harrisburg from the Pennsylvania perspective, see Robert Grant Crist, "Highwater 1863: The Confederate Approach to Harrisburg," *Pennsylvania History: A Journal of Mid-Atlantic Studies* 30, no. 2 (April 1963): pp.158–183.

10. For an excellent discussion of the regiment at Gettysburg, see Michael Taylor, "Ramseur's Brigade in the Gettysburg Campaign: A Newly Discovered Account by Capt. James I. Harris, Co. I, 30th Regt. N.C.T.," *Gettysburg* 17: pp. 26–40.

11. William Sillers (near Darksville, Va.) to his sister (North Carolina) 16 July 1863.

12. Louis M. Wicker was 30 when he enlisted on 15 August 1861. He mustered in as sergeant and was reduced to ranks in December 1862. Killed 1 July 1863.

13. A.F. Harrington (Orange Court House, Virginia) to John Harrington (Harnett County, N.C.) 10 August 1863.

14. Ardrey, *Diary*, 12 July 1863.

15. Alfred C. Young III, *Lee's Army During the Overland Campaign: A*

Numerical Study. Baton Rouge: Louisiana State University Press, 2013, p. 281, gives the following as casualty numbers for the 30th in May 1864: killed in action 36; wounded in action 114; wounded and captured 7; missing 96. This gives 253 total casualties. He evidently counted deserters and AWOL as missing. They were certainly not MIA. His number of wounded, 114, is completely unjustified by the available sources.

16. Ardrey, *Diary*, 21 July 1864.

17. Glatthaar, *Soldiering*, p. 31 shows 27.1 percent of infantrymen in the Army of Northern Virginia died.

18. In the 1850 census, Jones was employed as a bank cashier with personal property of $2,000. He was married with two children.

19. Casualties varied enormously from regiment to regiment. The 55th North Carolina suffered 15.4 percent dead of disease; 10.8 percent killed in action; 1 percent missing in action; 23 percent wounded; 23 percent captured. Jeffrey M. Girvan, *The 55th North Carolina in the Civil War*. Jefferson, NC: McFarland, 2006.

20. Jarratt Graham (Company H) was wounded at Gaines Mill and then sent home on wounded furlough. After arriving by train in Wilmington, he boarded a boat to travel upriver to Fayetteville. Apparently he fell overboard and drowned on 4 July 1862. (National Archives, Personal Jacket Jarratt Graham). James D. White enlisted at the age of 27 on 10 August 1861. In late March 1863, he deserted. On 10 January 1864, he was killed resisting arrest. (National Archives, Personal Jacket James D. White)

21. On this point I must be skeptical of Professor Glatthaar's numbers. He shows 13.7 percent combat deaths and only 12.7 percent dead of disease.

22. This is almost identical with Professor Glatthaar's wounded in the infantry of the Army of Northern Virginia: 30.7 percent.

23. B.C. Jackson (Chimborazo Hospital, Richmond) to Effie Jackson (Moore County, N.C.) 22 July 1863. Jackson Letters.

24. J.B. Ellen was 17 when he volunteered in September 1861. He was promoted to sergeant 20 August 1862. He is not found in the 1860 census but in 1850 was a boy living with his father, a farmer with no property.

25. The full description can be found in *MSHWR*, I, II, 579.

26. James N. Fuller, aged 18, mustered into Company G on 7 September 1861; promoted to corporal on 22 September 1862; promoted to sergeant 8 August 1863. In 1860, he lived with his father, a farmer with $1,500 real estate and $13,000 personal property, mostly 12 slaves. After his wounded furlough, he was retired to the Invalid Corps on 14 February 1865.

27. National Archives, Personal Jacket James N. Fuller.

28. *MSHWR*.

29. *MSHWR*, Vol I, part 2, p. 356.

30. *MSHWR*, Vol I, part 2, p. 326.

31. Glatthaar, *Soldiering*, p. 31 reports 14.3 percent of infantrymen in the Army of Northern Virginia were captured.

32. *Ibid.* gives an overall casualty rate in infantrymen of the Army of Northern Virginia of 68.7 percent.

Chapter 8

1. It was only toward the end of the war that the Union made considerable progress in identifying its dead and in establishing cemeteries. The Confederate Army never made substantial improvement. For an excellent discussion of the problems during the war in both armies, see Drew Gilpin Faust, ""The Dread Void of Uncertainty": Naming the Dead in the American Civil War," *Southern Cultures* 11, no. 2 (2005): pp. 7–32.

2. There is a list of deceased soldiers for the last quarter of 1861 in National Archives, Personal Jacket John C. Simmons. Simmons is the first man on the list.

3. For example, Private Levi Jarvis of Company C died 20 May 1863 at Chimborazo and was still listed as absent in hospital on company records as late as

September 1863. J.J. Pegram was listed AWOL for several months because the surgeon of the hospital where he was did not bother to report his presence. National Archives, Personal Jackets Levi Jarvis and J.J. Pegram.

4. *The Fayetteville Observer* (Fayetteville, N.C.), 16 March 1863, printed a list of the deaths in Company H through 7 March 1863.

5. Jacob Gaster (Rollins Store, Moore County, N.C.) to Chimborazo (Richmond, Va.) 30 July 1863. National Archives, Personal Jacket John C Gaster.

6. National Archives, Personal Jacket James A. Hunt.

7. The exchange of letters quoted by Carol C. Green, *Chimborazo: the Confederacy's Largest Hospital*. Knoxville: University of Tennessee Press, 2004, pp. 29–30.

8. Captain John Witherspoon (Camp below Fredericksburg) to Maj Gen D.H. Hill (Richmond) 3 January 1863. National Archives, Personal Jacket Robert Wolfe.

9. National Archives, Personal Jacket Hartwell Butler.

10. The regiment was formed in October 1861, but one company had been formed in April.

11. Men captured from the 58th North Carolina mostly were sent to Rock Island, Illinois. Michael Hardy describes the prison camp and the many deaths resulting from conditions there. Hardy, *Fifty-eighth*, pp. 94–96.

12. In both armies, deaths from disease greatly outnumbered deaths from combat. This was not at all the case in many Union regiments where the opposite was true. For example, in the 58th Massachusetts, disease killed 156 and combat 139. In the 20th Massachusetts, 260 died from combat and 149 from disease. For information on 300 Union regiments, see William F. Fox, *Regimental Losses in the American Civil War 1861–1865*. Albany, NY: Albany Publishing Company, 1889.

13. On the one point of disease deaths versus combat deaths, I will express considerable skepticism on the validity of Glatthaar's sample. In his sample

of infantrymen in the Army of Northern Virginia, 13.7 percent were killed in action and 12.7 percent died of disease. Only more detailed research can say if his numbers are accurate. However, on the surface they are dubious and fly in the face of all assumptions about disease versus combat in pre-20th-century wars and certainly are vastly different from numbers for the 30th North Carolina. Glatthaar, *Soldiering*, p. 31, Figure 2.8.

Chapter 9

1. William H. Bradford enlisted in Company G on 7 September 1861 and was listed absent sick for the rest of the month. He died in Raleigh of typhoid fever 18 October 1861, never having reached the unit. National Archives, Personal Jacket William Bradford.

2. For example, Dr. J.M. Campbell was often with Company H. He was born in 1835, lived in the Buffalo section of Moore County (now Lee County). In 1860, he lived with E.H. Cook, a 45-year-old woman who was perhaps his housekeeper and owned $2,000 in personal property.

3. *North Carolina Troops* gives the names of many of these men. We have not included them in this study because they were never a part of the unit.

4. General debility, 12 men; discharged, no reason given but certainly health, nine men; tuberculous variously described, eight men; chronic rheumatism, almost certainly malaria, seven men; injuries, four men; hernias, three men; heart disease, two men; insanity, two men; one man each *caxalgia*, spinal disease, gonorrhea, cancer of the stomach, tuberculous of the throat, typhoid fever.

5. The actual loss of personnel was worse than 10 percent. Eight men transferred to other units; 26 (mostly officers not reelected in April-May 1862) had resigned; eight provided substitutes and left.

6. Ross was a 28-year-old farmer when he enrolled in Company G in March 1862. In 1860, he owned personal

property valued at $100 and was married with three children.

7. Three cases of acute diarrhea and 44 of chronic.

8. J.G. Witherspoon (Camp Wyatt) to Hassie Witherspoon (Mecklenburg County, N.C.) 17 November 1861. Witherspoon Letters.

9. There were apparently several different diseases circulating including measles, German measles and roseola and perhaps chicken pox.

10. For an interesting discussion of how physicians learned from the war and improved the quality of medicine during the war, see Kathryn Shively Meier, "« Notre Devoir Envers La Science »". Médecines Humaine Et Animale Dans La Guerre De Sécession, 1861–1865." *Le Mouvement Social*, no. 257 (2016): pp. 47–69. www.jstor.org/stable/26321988.

11. A good book to read on the struggles of some physicians to introduce sterilization and anesthesia to 19th-century medicine is the delightful *Dr. Mutter's Marvels* by Cristin O'Keefe Aptowicz. New York: Gotham Books, 2014.

12. For a good, concise account of medicine in both armies, including what was done correctly, see Michael A. Flannery, "Civil War Pharmacy and Medicine: Comparisons and Contexts," *Pharmacy in History* 46, no. 2 (2004): pp. 71–80. www.jstor.org/stable/41112722.

13. B.C. Jackson (Winder Hospital, Richmond) to A.A. Jackson (Moore County, N.C.) 19 November 1862. Jackson Letters.

14. J.G. Witherspoon (Fredericksburg, Virginia) to Hassie Witherspoon (Mecklenburg County, N.C.) 22 December 1862. Witherspoon Letters.

15. B.C. Jackson (Winder Hospital, Richmond) to A.A. Jackson (Moore County, N.C.) 19 November 1862. Jackson Letters.

16. *MSHWR.*

17. *MSHWR*, Vol I, part 3, p. 74.

18. For an interesting discussion of which mosquitoes cause the different fevers and the reasons that terian fever is a 48-hour fever schedule and quartan a 72-hour fever schedule, see Timothy C.

Wingard, *The Mosquito: A Human History of Our Deadliest Predator.* New York: Dutton, 2019, p. 48.

19. Lt. A.A. Jackson was hospitalized for small pox but, since he evidently suffered a mild case, was more concerned with his suffering from "rumatic pains very badly in deed & I feel stiff in my joints yet but the pains has abated considerable." A.A. Jackson (Small Pox Hospital at Guinee Station, Va.) to Effie Jackson (Moore County, N.C.) 26 March 1863. Jackson Letters.

20. *MSHWR*, Vol I, part 3, p. 78.

21. Hornaday was 31 years old, a native of Moore County, and enlisted in Company H in August 1862 following the draft. In 1860, he was a farmer with no real estate and $200 of personal property, married with two children. He was furloughed from mid-June 1862 to 10 July 1862 to recover from malaria. His hospital stay for rheumatism was four months ending on 17 January 1863. He was a POW when the war ended.

22. National Archives, Personal Jacket W.H. Brown.

23. National Archives, Personal Jacket Henry Brinkley.

24. Griffin was a 22-year-old man living with his father—a farmer with $1,550 of real estate and $1,221 of personal property in 1860—when he enlisted in Company I in September 1861.

25. This was Louis McLeod whose letters home have been referred to so often in this study.

26. A.F. Harrington (Camp near Brandy Station, Va.) to John Harrington (Harnett County, N.C.) 7 November 1863.

27. Louis McLeod (Camp Wyatt) to Eliza McLeod (Moore County, N.C.) 26 January 1862.

28. Graham was a native of Ireland, 45 years old when he enlisted in Company H in August 1861. Missed in the 1860 census.

29. National Archives, Personal Jacket Z.R. Roberson. Private Roberson was assigned to duty with Company G on 10 June 1864.

30. Smith is not listed in the 1860 census, and we know nothing about him

except that he was 44 years old, from Warren County, probably a farmer when he enlisted in Company B in August 1861.

31. Robinson was an unmarried man living with his father—a farm laborer with personal property of $150—when he enlisted in Company K in September 1861.

32. This omits outliers of 1, 508 and 602 days. Including them raised the average stay to 49 days.

33. D. McLeod (Lynchburg, Va.) to Effie Jackson (Moore County, N.C.) 2 December 1862. Jackson Letters.

34. Louis McLeod (Camp Wyatt) to Eliza McLeod (Moore County, N.C.) 2 December 1861.

35. Denson was a 19-year-old living with his father—a farmer with $600 of real estate and $587 of personal property in 1860—when he enlisted in Company I in September 1861. He was exchanged as a POW on 3 March 1865 and was either hospitalized or simply slipped away. There are no records for him after his exchange.

36. Batchelor was an illiterate man of 23 when he enlisted in Company I from Nash County in September 1861.

37. Mashburn was 21 years old living in Moore County when he enlisted in Company H in August 1861. He was missed in the 1860 census.

38. Icterus and jaundice could have referred to malarial symptoms.

39. Autry was a 21-year-old, illiterate turpentine laborer, owning no property when he enlisted in Company A in September 1861.

40. Private Alexander S. Robinson (Company C) was superficially wounded and captured at Gettysburg. He was admitted to prison hospital on 8 November 1863, suffering from scurvy. The posterior and inner aspect of the right thigh and the calf of the right leg were extensively discolored with purple spots. Treatment: tincture of iodine was applied externally and chlorate of potash prescribed for internal use. Importantly, a full diet was ordered. By 20 November, the spots had disappeared and he was nearly well though there remained some dropsical swelling of foot and leg

for which a mixture of squill, buchu and sweet spirit of nitre was administered. On 3 March 1864, he was sent for exchange. Information found in *MSHWR*, I, III, 700.

41. Vomiting of blood can indicate several different conditions. In these cases, perhaps damage due to excessive alcohol consumption.

42. Since some hospitals were known by several names, it is difficult to have an exact number. For a full list, see https://www.civilwarrichmond.com/hospital-lists/206-index-of-hospitals-in-richmond-va-during-the-civil-war.

43. National Archives, Personal Jacket Willis N. Bowlin.

44. For detail on Chimborazo as well as some information on other hospitals in Richmond, see Carol C. Green, *Chimborazo: the Confederacy's Largest Hospital*. Knoxville: University of Tennessee Press, 2004. A superb study of Civil War hospitals in general is Margaret Humphreys, *Marrow of Tragedy: The Health Crisis of the American Civil War*. Baltimore: John Hopkins Press, 2013.

45. J.W. Brassfield (Richmond, Va.) to Jesse Goodin (Wake County, N.C.) 24 July 1862. Goodin Letters.

Chapter 10

1. Louis McLeod (Camp Holmes) to Eliza McLeod (Moore County, N.C.) 13 April 1862.

2. Horace Morrison was a 23-year-old farmer when he enlisted in Moore County in August 1861. He was wounded at Malvern Hill 1 July 1862 and killed 8 May 1864.

3. Louis McLeod (Camp Holmes) to Eliza McLeod (Moore County, N.C.) 4 April 1862.

4. Ardrey, *Diary*, 17 September 1862.

5. William Sillers (Camp in Virginia) to his sister (North Carolina) 1 October 1862. Sillers Letters.

6. Ardrey, *Diary*, 14 October 1862.

7. William Sillers (near Strasburg, Va.) to his sister (North Carolina) 15 November 1862. Sillers Letters.

8. J.W. Brassfield (Hamilton's Crossing,

Va.) to Jesse Goodin (Wake County, N.C.) 20 March 1863. Goodin Letters.

9. Francis Parker (Virginia) to Sara Parker (Halifax County, N.C.) 19 April 1863. Parker, *Letters*, p. 238.

10. Francis Parker (Virginia) to Sara Parker (Halifax County, N.C.) 25 April 1863. Parker, *Letters*, p. 242.

11. Francis Parker (Virginia) to Sara Parker (Halifax County, N.C.) 10 May 1863. Parker, *Letters*, p. 275.

12. Ardrey, *Diary*, April 1863.

13. B.C. Jackson (Camp at Hamilton's Crossing, Va.) to A.A. Jackson (home on furlough) 25 April 1863. Jackson Letters.

14. A.A. Jackson (Camp near Fredericksburg, Va.) to Effie Jackson (Moore County, N.C.) 15 May 1863. Jackson Letters.

15. B.C. Jackson (Caroline County, Va.) to Effie Jackson (Moore County, N.C.) 23 March 1863. Jackson Letters.

16. Dougald C. Shaw was a 22-year-old farm laborer when he enlisted in August 1861. In 1860, he lived on the farm where he was employed. He owned no property. He was hospitalized for an unrecorded illness in September 1862; in November 1862, he was admitted to Chimborazo with typhoid (*Febris contin commonis*); he was captured at Antietam and exchanged a month later; he was wounded and captured a second time at Kelly's Ford in November 1863. He spent the remainder of the war in various federal prison camps, treated for small pox from 8 Feb to 8 March 1864. He was freed in June 1865 after swearing the oath of loyalty to the United States.

17. D.C. Shaw (Camp in Virginia) to Effie Jackson (Moore County, N.C.) 30 March 1863. Jackson Letters.

18. A.F. Harrington (Orange County Court House, Va.) to John Harrington (Harnett County, N.C.) 7 April 1863.

19. Rufus D. Stallings (Virginia) to Elizabeth Ward (Rocky Mount) 18 August 1863. Stallings Letters.

20. For this view, see articles by Richard Bardolph, "Inconstant Rebels: Desertion of North Carolina Troops in the Civil War," *North Carolina Historical Review* 41 (Spring 1964): pp. 163–189; "Confederate

Dilemma: North Carolina Troops and the Deserter Problem," *North Carolina Historical Review* 66 (1989), January: pp. 61–86, April: pp. 179–210.

21. Richard Reid, "A Test Case of the "Crying Evil": Desertion among North Carolina Troops during the Civil War," *The North Carolina Historical Review* 58, no. 3 (1981): pp. 234–62. This statistical study should be the starting point for general statements on overall deserters among North Carolina troops. Reid concludes that desertions were strongest in areas occupied by the Union and that "class stratification was a significant factor." p. 247.

22. Sheehan-Dean, *Confederates*, pp. 95, 165.

23. Katherine A. Giuffre, "First in Flight: Desertion as Politics in the North Carolina Confederate Army," *Social Science History* 21, no. 2 (Summer 1997): pp. 245–263.

24. Peter S. Bearman, a sociologist, used the same sample data as Giuffre and concluded that there was no evidence whatsoever that desertions had to do with harvest. It is a classic example of conclusions varying depending on how data is arranged. Giuffre broke out desertions by month which shows a strong tendency to desert at harvest and planting times. Bearman broke out desertions by quarter and the monthly differences were smoothed out showing no correlation to harvest time. Peter S. Bearman, "Desertion as Localism: Army Unit Solidarity and Group Norms in the U.S. Civil War," *Social Forces* 70, no. 2 (1991): pp. 321–42. His one firm conclusion is that late in the war companies composed of men from the same county or place saw higher desertion than more heterogeneous companies. In short, local identities were far more important than Confederate nationalist identity. The men of the 30th tend to confirm this view.

25. *Ibid.* p. 260.

26. John Louis Cox was the son of a prosperous farmer with real estate of $2,000 and personal property of $15,000, including 11 slaves. He was 21 when he volunteered in August 1861. He was

wounded at Malvern Hill 1 July 1862 and twice detailed to catch deserters. In June 1864, he was transferred to the Invalid Corps.

27. National Archives, Personal Jackets J.L. Cox and James P. Deaton.

28. He was delivered to Camp Holmes on 29 October 1863. National Archives, Personal Jacket Bennett Crumpler.

29. National Archives, Personal Jacket Charles L. Goebel.

30. J.W. Brassfield (Camp in Virginia) to Jesse Goodin (Wake County, N.C.) 30 May 1863. Goodin Letters.

31. J.C. Goodin (Camp in Virginia) to Jesse Goodin (Wake County, N.C.) 25 June 1863. Goodin Letters.

32. Rufus Stallings (Camp on the road in Virginia) to Elizabeth Ward (Rocky Mount) 16 September 1863. Stallings Letters.

33. A.A. Jackson (Camp near Kelly's Ford, Va.) to Effie Jackson (Moore County, N.C.) 26 October 1863. Jackson Letters.

34. Neither *North Carolina Troops* nor Archival Jackets mentions a Pegram becoming lieutenant in Company B so it is possible that the election was not confirmed by higher authorities. This would have been either Mitchell Pegram or Robert B. Pegram.

35. Ardrey, *Diary*, 1–10 December 1863.

36. James T. Lee was 23 when he enlisted in September 1861. He was the 1st sergeant of Company K. He is missing from the census records. Hospitalized for typhoid pneumonia December 1862–3 February 1863. He was killed on 12 May 1864.

37. John N. Black was 26 years old when he joined Company K in October 1861. He was promoted to sergeant. In 1860, he was an unmarried farmer with $2,900 of real property and $6,000 of personal property, including six slaves. He was killed on 18 July 1864.

38. Ardrey, *Diary*, 25 December 1863.

39. R.K.B. Thomas (Camp in Virginia) to Jesse Goodin (Wake County, N.C.) 5 December 1863. Goodin Letters.

40. William Sillers (Camp near Hamilton's Crossing, Va.) to Almond Holmes (North Carolina) 9 Feb 1863. Sillers Letters.

41. William Sillers (Camp near Hamilton's Crossing) to his sister (North Carolina) 26 Feb 1863. Sillers Letters.

42. Ardrey, *Diary*, 30 October 1863.

43. Harrell mustered in as 1st sergeant, aged 19, on 31 August 1861 and on 10 March 1862 was elected 1st lieutenant of Company F. In 1860, he was living with his father who was a farmer with $3,000 of real property and $3,000 of personal property. He was wounded in the run up to Antietam, returning to duty in January 1863. *North Carolina Troops* does not indicate that he was promoted to Field and Staff, but he signed the 31 March 1864 receipt as Assistant QM 30th North Carolina. Also, Lieutenant Archibald Jackson in one of his letters home refers to Harrell as the QM for the regiment. He was killed 12 May 1864.

44. National Archives, Personal Jacket George K. Harrell.

45. James Rogers was a native of Scotland, occupation miner, who volunteered at age 22 in August 1861. He was captured 12 May 1864 at Spotsylvania Court House. He was released in June 1864 when he joined the 1st Regiment of U.S. Volunteer Infantry.

46. A.F. Harrington (Camp near Meador Ford, Va.) to John A. McDonald (Harnett County, N.C.) 4 January 1864.

47. Rufus D. Stallings (Camp in Virginia) to Elizabeth Ward (Rocky Mount) 31 January 1864. Stallings Letters.

48. John A. McDonald (Orange Court House, Va.) to John Harrington (Harnett County, N.C.) 10 February 1864.

49. James L. Green (near Orange Court House, Va.) to Mary Green (Cleveland County, N.C.) 29 April 1864. Green Letters.

50. J.R. Hunter lived in Union County and was conscripted at the age of 40 in September 1863. He deserted on 28 February 1864.

51. James L. Green (Virginia) to Mary Green (Cleveland County, N.C.) 4 March 1864. Green Letters.

52. Joseph Goodin (Lynchburg, Va.)

to Jesse Goodin (Wake County, N.C.) 28 June 1864. Goodin Letters.

53. Joseph Goodin (Camp near Petersburg, Va.) to Jesse Goodin (Wake County, N.C.) 24 December 1864. Goodin Letters.

54. Men had been executed for desertion before. In 1862, Jackson ordered the execution of three men. Peter Carmichael described the Jackson executions and other punishments in a fine article. Included are pictures and sketches made by soldiers of some of the punishments including "bucking." Peter S. Carmichael, "So Far from God and So Close to Stonewall Jackson: The Executions of Three Shenandoah Valley Soldiers," *The Virginia Magazine of History and Biography* 111, no. 1 (2003): pp. 33–66. www.jstor.org/stable/4250076.

55. Joseph Goodin (Virginia) to Jesse Goodin (Wake County, N.C.) 1 May 1864. Goodin Letters.

56. James L. Green (Camp near Orange Court House, Va.) to Mary Green (Cleveland County, N.C.) 29 April 1864. Green Letters.

57. Ardrey, *Diary*, 29 April 1864.

58. James L. Green (Camp near Orange Court House, Va.) to Mary Green (Cleveland County, N.C.) 29 April 1864. Green Letters.

59. A good summary of North Carolina's lack of support for the Confederacy, often openly hostile, is found in Archie K. Davis, ""She Disdains to Pluck One Laurel from a Sister's Brow": Disloyalty to the Confederacy in North Carolina," *The Virginia Magazine of History and Biography* 88, no. 2 (1980): pp. 131–47. www.jstor.org/stable/4248383. The tone of the article fits the "lost cause" mentality and seeks to defend North Carolina's devotion to the cause. However, the summary of North Carolina unhappiness with the Confederacy, and the reasons for it, is clear and well done.

60. A.F. Harrington (Orange County Court House, Virginia) to John Harrington (Harnett County, N.C.) 10 August 1863.

61. A.F. Harrington (Orange County Court House, Virginia) to John Harrington (Harnett County, N.C.) 11 September 1863.

62. Horace W. Raper, "William W. Holden and the Peace Movement in North Carolina," *The North Carolina Historical Review* 31, no. 4 (1954): pp. 493–516. www.jstor.org/stable/23516160.

63. A.A. Jackson (Camp in Virginia) to his family (Moore County, N.C.) 5 April 1864. Jackson Letters.

64. Richard Bardolph, "Inconstant Rebels: Desertion of North Carolina Troops in the Civil War," *North Carolina Historical Review* 41 (2): pp. 175–176. This fine analysis of the rate of desertion among North Carolina troops was written during the centennial of the Civil War. It is interesting today to read history with such an overtly pro-Confederate slant.

65. North Carolina State Archives, Personal Collection 286. All but one of the letters have been edited by Joyce E. Agerton and published in *The Guilford County Genealogical Society* 27, no. 2 (Spring 2000): pp. 69–77.

66. John J. Armfield was a 35-year-old Quaker from Guilford County, a gunsmith when he was conscripted in the fall of 1864. In 1860, he was married with one child and owned real estate valued at $1,000 and personal property of $300. He was captured in the spring of 1865 and died of acute dysentery while a POW. As a Quaker, he should have been exempt from conscription.

67. John L. Shearin was a 19-year-old farmer living in Warren County when he enrolled in August of 1862. A small man—5'5"—he was not in good health and was hospitalized three times—typhoid, pneumonia and epistaxis—in the spring of 1862. As a result he was discharged on 22 May 1862 but re-enlisted on 16 July 1863. He was captured at Kelly's Ford, released, wounded in September 1864, wounded in the face on the eve of the surrender at Appomattox Court House and was paroled several days after the surrender.

68. North Carolina Archives. Reminiscences of John L. Sherrin.

69. Inspection report for Cox's brigade, 25 February 1865, National

Archives, Record Group 109, Microcopy 935, Roll 15, 6-P.62. Cited by Taylor, *Parker Letters*, p. 361.

70. Joseph Goodin (near Petersburg, Va.) to Jesse Goodin (Wake County, N.C.) 23 March 1865.

71. Clifford Dowdy, *Lee's Last Campaign: The Story of Lee & His Men against Grant—1864*. Lincoln: University of Nebraska Press, 1993, p. 375.

72. A.F. Harrington (near Petersburg, Va.) to John Harrington (Harnett County, N.C.) 6 March 1865.

73. Robert Matthew Crumpler was 20 years old, a teacher in Sampson County when he enrolled in Company A in September 1861. He was later promoted to 1st sergeant. In 1860, he was living with his father, a farmer, who owned real estate valued at $6,000 and personal property of $100 and two slaves. He was wounded four times during the war. He surrendered with the unit at Appomattox Court House.

74. North Carolina Archives: ORG 141.4, Folder 2. UDC: Papers of Georgia Hicks: Typed excerpts from the War Diary of R.M. Crumpler, Clinton, N.C.

Conclusion

1. A.F. Harrington (near Petersburg, Va.) to John Harrington (Harnett County, N.C.) 6 March 1865.

2. William Sillers (Virginia) to his sister (North Carolina) 16 July 1863. Sillers Letters.

3. A.F. Harrington (near Petersburg, Va.) to John Harrington (Harnett County, N.C.) 6 March 1865.

4. Sheehan-Dean, *Confederates*, p. 191, points out a handful of Virginians in the Shenandoah who were tempted to continue to fight.

Appendix

1. Weymouth T. Jordan, Jr, Ed., *North Carolina Troops 1861–1865 a Roster.* Vol VIII *Infantry, 27th-31st Regiments.* Raleigh: North Carolina Office of Archives and History, 2004.

2. RG109 War Department. Collection Confederate Records. PI 101, Entry 18. Boxes 741, 742, 743 muster rolls and pay rolls for the various companies of 30th North Carolina.

3. Considering the massive number of documents, it is inevitable that there is some confusion over identification and that in the process of microfilming some documents were placed out of order. Nevertheless, the personal jackets are the most important resource for any research on individual men.

4. Louis McLeod in letters to his wife dated from September 1861 through June 1862.

5. Francis Parker (near Richmond, Va.) to his wife (Tarboro, N.C.) 24 July 1862. Parker, *Letters*, p. 201.

6. Joseph J. Goodin enlisted in Wake County at the age of 20 on 20 March 1864. His brother John C. (Company D) died at Gettysburg, his brother Willis N. (Company D) died of typhoid fever on 30 August 1862 and his half-brother James Wesley Brassfield (Company D) died while a prisoner of war on 12 February 1864. The father Jesse B. Goodin (or Goodwin) was a Wake County farmer owning $400 of real estate and $575 of personal property in 1860.

7. William W. Cooper enlisted 10 August 1861 at the age of 20. He was wounded in the right arm at Antietam, wounded in the head at Winchester, Virginia, on 9 November 1864. He returned to duty early in 1865, was captured on 6 April 1865 and released on 26 June 1865 after taking the oath of allegiance.

8. J.J. Goodin (Winchester, Va.) to J.C. Goodin (Raleigh, N.C.) 14 July 1864. Goodin Letters.

9. Francis R. Canady enlisted in Company D on 10 September 1863 at the age of 43. He was captured on 22 September 1864 and received at James River, Virginia, for exchange on 21 January 1865. There is no record that he ever rejoined the regiment. Canady lived in Wake County and was a farm laborer with personal property of $40 in 1860.

10. John King enlisted on 1 April 1864 at the age of 28. Hospitalized at Raleigh

in October 1864; captured on 6 April 1865; died while a prisoner of war on 29 May 1865. He was by occupation a stone mason living in Wake County in 1860.

11. Francis Canady (Charlottesville, Va.) to Jesse Goodin (Raleigh, N.C.) 23 July 1864. Goodin Letters.

12. These numbers are based on muster rolls in North Carolina State Archives.

13. Louis McLeod (near Richmond) to Eliza McLeod (Moore County, N.C.) 22 June 1862.

14. On the various conscription laws, see Mitchell, *Conscription*, pp. 23–70.

15. Only one man, Daniel Hinshaw, was discharged from the 30th on this ground. In 1860, he lived in Chatham County with his father who was a farmer with $200 in personal property. Hinshaw was inducted 15 July 1863 and discharged 24 November 1863.

16. An interesting discussion of conflict over conscription and resistance to it in central North Carolina can be found in William R. Trotter, *Silk Flags and Cold Steel: The Civil War in North Carolina: The Piedmont*. Winston-Salem: John F. Blair, 1988, pp. 145–162.

17. Mitchell cites a report that in January 1864 North Carolina had 80,957 men in the field with 38,166 declared exempt for all reasons. Only 12,877 men were unaccounted for.

18. Rufus D. Stallings (Camp in Virginia) to Elizabeth Ward (Rocky Mount, N.C.) 29 December 1863. Stallings Letters.

19. Lawrence Battle enlisted 5 January 1862. He was a prosperous farmer in 1860 with real property valued at $12,555

and personal property of $32,675, including 28 slaves. He was married with no children. He served until 1 September 1862 when he paid William Bass to serve in his place. Bass joined Company I on 4 December 1862 at the age of 52 and died of pneumonia in March 1863, leaving five young children. Battle seems to have provided for the children. Battle was later named conscript officer for Franklin County with the task of enrolling conscripts and finding deserters. When he was ordered back into uniform in 1864 he wrote, and solicited from others, many letters about why he was needed in Nash County. In addition to his duties, he was the only overseer over 20 able-bodied Negroes (total of 47 or 48 slaves on the plantation), suffered from rheumatism, and cleared the county of deserters despite attempts on his life. See National Archives, Personal Jacket L.F. Battle for the letters.

20. See Chapter 5, that several men of color were enrolled in the 30th North Carolina in the fall of 1861.

21. National Archives, Personal Jacket J.N. Ballenton. Also cited in *North Carolina Troops*, VII, p. 332.

22. Our numbers are confirmed as being very close by two inspections carried out on 29 January and 25 February 1865. The former showed 10 officers and 167 men present with three officers and 42 men absent without leave. The second inspection listed five officers and 176 men present and three officers and 49 men absent without leave. Inspections reports for Cox's brigade, National Archives. Cited by Taylor, *Parker Letters*, p. 361.

Bibliography

Primary Sources: Archival and Unpublished

Private Collections

Letters written by Louis H. McLeod and his wife Eliza Walker McLeod in the possession of Annie Thomas, a family member, of Broadway, N.C. I was permitted to copy these letters in the 1960s. The letters are rich in description of life in military camps of 1861 and 1862 and detail about the life of one North Carolina rural family—without husband—and how it survived on the farm. The letters are very special in that both sides of the correspondence have been preserved with only a few gaps. The wife kept most of her husband's letters and he kept hers. Louis wrote his first letter on 19 September 1861, and Eliza wrote her first letter around 20 September 1861. When McLeod returned home in the summer of 1862, after being gravely wounded in the battle of Malvern Hill, most of her letters to him returned home with him and have been preserved. In addition, McLeod kept some letters from his brother-in-law, who had volunteered for the 2nd N.C. Cavalry and from other friends.

Letters from Louis H. McLeod, A.F. Harrington, J.K.P. Harrington, John A. MacDonald and others written to Mr. John Harrington of Harnett County, N.C. The letters were kept by the family in a trunk now in the possession of family member Dixie Perez of Broadway, N.C. I copied the letters in the 1960s.

One letter from A.F. Harrington to John A. McDonald given to me by McDonald's grandson, Mr. Leon M. McDonald of Olivia, N.C.

Letters in Possession of the 30th North Carolina Reenactment Unit

Letters of John G. Witherspoon transcribed with notes on persons mentioned by Dorothy Deal Rogers.

Letters to and from Mary Griffin Green, 1859–1866. Her husband, James L. Green, was assigned to Company H of the 30th North Carolina. *North Carolina Troops* indicates that James L. Green joined in August 1863, but it is very clear from the letters that he was present at least a year earlier.

Archival Collections

Davidson College Archives

Diaries of William E. Ardrey. Accessible online: https://davidsonarchivesandspecialcolle ctions.org/archives/digital-collections/ardrey-papers. The diaries are four manuscript volumes, one for each year, 1862–1865.

Bibliography

Duke University, Perkins Library, Special Collections

Jesse B. Goodin Papers. DO3570923T. Thirty-eight letters, mostly from J.W. Brassfield, John C. Goodin and Joseph Goodin to family.

John McLean Harrington Papers. Some letters from Abner Flynn Harrington to his brother James S. Harrington.

East Carolina University Archives

Rufus Delano Stallings letters. Accessible online: https://digital.lib.ecu.edu/3340.

National Archives, Washington, D.C.

RG109 War Department. Collection Confederate Records. PI 101, Entry 18. Boxes 741, 742, 743 muster rolls and pay rolls for the various companies of 30th North Carolina.

Record Group 109. Compiled Military Service Records, North Carolina. Notecards and original records are contained in folders or jackets for individuals. The jackets are organized by unit and are alphabetical within units. Available on microfilm and online through Ancestry.com and Fold3.

United States Census records.

North Carolina State Archives, Raleigh, North Carolina

Letters from John J. Armfield to his wife. Personal Collection 286. The collection consists of typed transcriptions of the letters. In addition, some letters from Armfield were published in *The Guilford Genealogist*, 27, No. 2 (Spring 2000).

Walter J. Bone Collection.

Bounty payrolls, Military Collection, Civil War:

    Company A, Sampson County. Box 11

    Company B, Warren County. Box 12

    Company D, Franklin County. Box 10; Granville County. Box 10; Wake County. Box 12.

    Company H, Harnett County. Box 10

    Company I, Nash County. Box 11

    Company K, Mecklenburg County. Box 10

Crumpler, R.M. Typed copy of his diary for April 1865. North Carolina Archives. UDC, papers of Georgia Hicks. ORG 141.4, Folder 2.

Fitts, Frank M., A Sketch of My Life written 7 February 1914. North Carolina Archives. Military Collection, Civil War. Box 70, Folder 49.

Shearin, John L. Reminiscences of his experience late in the war. North Carolina Archives. Military Collection, Civil War. Box 72, Folder 7.

University of Notre Dame, Rare Book Collection

Jackson Family Correspondence, 1852–1866. Rare Book Collection of University of Notre Dame, South Bend, IN. Not yet available online. Archibald A. Jackson was a turpentine distiller in Moore County before 1861. He was elected lieutenant in Company H of the 30th North Carolina.

Sillers-Holmes/5025–15 MSN/CW. Rare Books and Special Collections, Hesburgh Libraries of Notre Dame. Fourteen Letters from William W. Sillers and others to Frances Sillers Holmes of Sampson County, N.C. Accessible online: http://www.rarebooks.nd.edu/digital/civil_war/letters/sillers-holmes/.

Published Primary Sources

Barnes, Woodward, et al., eds. *The Medical and Surgical History of the War of the Rebellion.* 2 volumes in 6 parts. Washington: Government Printing Office, 1870–1888.

Betts, A.D. *Experience of a Confederate Chaplain 1861–1864.* Reprinted by Eastern Digital Resources, Augusta, GA, 2001.

Brown, Matthew M., ed. *North Carolina Troops 1861–1865: A Roster,* Vol VIII. Raleigh: North Carolina Office of Archives and History, 1981.

"Company H Moore County Rifles," *Fayetteville Observer,* 4 April 1864 (Lost Souls).

"Deaths in Company H, 30th Regiment N.C.T. Up to March 7, 1863," *Fayetteville Observer,* 16 March 1863.

Early, Jubal A. *A Memoire of the Last Year of the War for Independence in the Confederate States of America.* Lynchburg, VA: Button, 1867.

French, Samuel Gibbs. *Two Wars: An Autobiography of Gen. Samuel G. French....* Nashville, TN: Confederate Veteran, 1910.

Harrington, Zeb D., and Martha. *To Bear Arms: Civil War Information from Local "Folks" Chatham County and Adjacent Counties.* Moncure, NC: Privately published, 1984. The authors assembled much information on soldiers and civilians from several counties in central North Carolina. Many of the letters mentioned above from L.H. McLeod, J.A. McDonald and A.F. Harrington are photocopied and included.

McGill, A.D. "Fighting to the End," *The Daily News and Observer,* Raleigh, NC, 11 April 1905, p. 5.

Mehegan, Julianne, and David Mehegan, eds. *Record of a Soldier in the Late War: The Confederate Memoir of John Wesley Bone.* Hingham, MA: Chinquapin Publishers, 2014.

Norman, William M. *A Portion of My Life; Being a Short & Imperfect History Written While a Prisoner of War on Johnson's Island, 1864.* Auckland, New Zealand: Pickle Partners Publishing, 2015.

Perry, Aldo S. *Civil War Courts-Martial of North Carolina Troops.* Jefferson, NC: McFarland, 2012.

Public Laws of the State of North Carolina passed by the General Assembly, at its Session of 1860-'61. Accessible online: https://digital.ncdcr.gov/digital/collection/p249901coll22/id/178470.

Rable, George C., ed. *A Southern Woman's Story: Phoebe Yates Pember.* Columbia: University of South Carolina Press, 2002.

Records of the War of the Rebellion, S1, IX, XX.

"The Sampson Rangers, Company A, 30th N.C.R.," *Fayetteville Observer,* 4 April 1864 (Lost Souls).

Taylor, Michael W. "Ramseur's Brigade in the Gettysburg Campaign: A Newly Discovered Account by Capt. James I. Harris, Co I, 30th Regt. N.C.T.," *The Gettysburg Magazine,* No. 17 (1997), pp. 26–40.

Taylor, Michael W., ed. *To Drive the Enemy from Southern Soil: The Letters of Col. Francis Marion Parker and the History of the 30th Regiment North Carolina Troops.* Dayton, OH: Morningside House, 1998.

Secondary Sources Consulted

Aptowicz, Cristin O'Keefe. *Dr. Mutter's Marvels.* New York: Gotham Books, 2014.

Bardolph, Richard. "Confederate Dilemma: North Carolina Troops and the Deserter Problem," *The North Carolina Historical Review* 66, no. 1 (1989): pp. 61–86; no. 2 (1989): pp. 179–210.

_____. "Inconstant Rebels: Desertion of North Carolina Troops in the Civil War," *The North Carolina Historical Review* 41, no. 2 (1964): pp. 163–89.

Bibliography

Barrett, John G. *The Civil War in North Carolina*. Chapel Hill: University of North Carolina Press, 1963.

Bearman, Peter S. "Desertion as Localism: Army Unit Solidarity and Group Norms in the U.S. Civil War," *Social Forces* 70, no. 2 (1991): pp. 321–42.

Bernstein, Steven. *The Confederacy's Last Northern Offensive: Jubal Early, the Army of the Valley and the Raid on Washington*. Jefferson, NC: McFarland, 2011.

Bridges, Hal. *Lee's Maverick General: Daniel Harvey Hill*. Lincoln: University of Nebraska Press, 1991.

Carmichael, Peter S. "So Far from God and So Close to Stonewall Jackson: The Executions of Three Shenandoah Valley Soldiers," *The Virginia Magazine of History and Biography* 111, no. 1 (2003): pp. 33–66. www.jstor.org/stable/4250076.

The Civil War Battlefield Guide. Second Edition. Boston: Houghton Mifflin, 1998.

Cooke, Robert J. *Wild, Wicked Wartime Wilmington: Being an Account of Murder, Malice and Other Assorted Mayhem in N. C.'s Largest City During the Civil War*. Wilmington, NC: Dram Tree Books, 2009.

Crist, Robert Grant. "Highwater 1863: The Confederate Approach to Harrisburg," *Pennsylvania History: A Journal of Mid-Atlantic Studies* 30, no. 2 (April 1963): pp. 158–183.

David, William C. *Jefferson Davis: The Man and His Hour*. New York: HarperCollins, 1991.

Davis, Archie K. "'She Disdains to Pluck One Laurel from a Sister's Brow': Disloyalty to the Confederacy in North Carolina," *The Virginia Magazine of History and Biography* 88, no. 2 (1980): pp. 131–47. www.jstor.org/stable/4248383.

Devine, Shauna. *Learning from the Wounded: The Civil War and the Rise of American Medical Science*. Chapel Hill: University of North Carolina Press, 2014.

Dowd, Clifford. *Lee and His Men at Gettysburg: The Death of a Nation*. New York: Skyhorse, 1958.

_____. *Lee's Last Campaign: The Story of Lee & His Men Against Grant—1864*. Lincoln: University of Nebraska Press, 1993.

_____. *The Seven Days: The Emergence of Robert E. Lee and the Dawn of a Legend*. New York: Skyhorse, 1964.

Doyle, Patrick J. "Replacement Rebels: Confederate Substitution and the Issue of Citizenship," *Journal of the Civil War Era* 8, no. 1 (2018): pp. 3–31.

Faust, Drew Gilpin. "'The Dread Void of Uncertainty': Naming the Dead in the American Civil War," *Southern Cultures* 11, no. 2 (2005): pp. 7–32. www.jstor.org/stable/26390983.

_____. *This Republic of Suffering: Death and the American Civil War*. New York: Vintage Books, 2009.

Fielding, Lawrence W. "War and Trifles: Sport in the Shadows of Civil War Army Life," *Journal of Sport History* 4, no. 2 (1977): pp. 151–68. www.jstor.org/stable/43609251.

Flannery, Michael A. "Civil War Pharmacy and Medicine: Comparisons and Contexts," *Pharmacy in History* 46, no. 2 (2004): pp. 71–80. www.jstor.org/stable/41112722.

Fox, William F. *Regimental Losses in the American Civil War*. Albany, NY: Albany Publishing Company, 1889.

Girvan, Jeffrey M. *The 55th North Carolina in the Civil War*. Jefferson, NC: McFarland, 2006.

Giuffre, Katherine A. "First in Flight: Desertion as Politics in the North Carolina Confederate Army," *Social Science History* 21, no. 2 (Summer 1997): pp. 245–263.

Glatthaar, Joseph T. *Soldiering in the Army of Northern Virginia: A Statistical Portrait of the Troops Who Served Under Robert E. Lee*. Chapel Hill: University of North Carolina Press, 2011.

Green, Carol C. *Chimborazo: The Confederacy's Largest Hospital*. Knoxville: University of Tennessee Press, 2004.

Bibliography

Gwynne, S. C. *Rebel Yell: The Violence, Passion, and Redemption of Stonewall Jackson.* New York: Scribner's, 2014.

Hadley, Wade H., Jr. *The Story of the Cape Fear and Deep River Navigation Company 1849–1873.* Siler City, NC: Chatham County Historical Society, 1980.

Hale, Douglas. "The Third Texas Cavalry: A Socioeconomic Profile of a Confederate Regiment," *Military History of the Southwest* 19 (Spring 1989): pp. 1–26.

Hardy, Michael. *The Fifty-Eighth North Carolina Troops: Tar Heels in the Army of Tennessee.* Jefferson, NC: McFarland, 2010.

Harrell, Roger H. *The 2nd North Carolina Cavalry.* Jefferson, NC: McFarland, 2004.

Humphreys, Margaret. *Marrow of Tragedy: The Health Crisis of the American Civil War.* Baltimore: Johns Hopkins University Press, 2013.

Johnson, Guion Griffis. *Ante-Bellum North Carolina: A Social History.* Chapel Hill: University of North Carolina Press, 1937.

Jones, Terry L. "Wharf-Rats, Cutthroats and Thieves: The Louisiana Tigers, 1861–1862," *Louisiana History: The Journal of the Louisiana Historical Association* 27, no. 2 (1986): pp. 147–65. www.jstor.org/stable/4232496.

Lefler, Hugh, and Albert Newsome. *The History of a Southern State: North Carolina.* Chapel Hill: University of North Carolina Press, 1954.

Levin, Kevin. *Searching for Black Confederates: The Civil War's Most Persistent Myth.* Chapel Hill: University of North Carolina Press, 2019.

Marvel, William. *Lincoln's Mercenaries: Economic Motivation Among Union Soldiers During the Civil War.* Baton Rouge: Louisiana State University Press, 2018.

McPherson, James M. *For Cause & Comrades: Why Men Fought in the Civil War.* New York: Oxford University Press, 1997.

Meier, Kathryn S. "'No Place for the Sick': Nature's War on Civil War Soldier Mental and Physical Health in the 1862 Peninsula and Shenandoah Valley Campaigns," *Journal of the Civil War Era* 1, no. 2 (2011): pp. 176–206. www.jstor.org/stable/26070113.

_____. "'Notre Devoir Envers La Science.' Médecines humaine et animale dans la guerre de sécession, 1861–1865." *Le mouvement social,* no. 257 (2016): pp. 47–69. www.jstor.org/stable/26321988.

Merritt, Keri Leigh. *Masterless Men: Poor Whites and Slavery in the Antebellum South.* Cambridge: Cambridge University Press, 2017.

Miller, Brian Craig. *Empty Sleeves: Amputation in the Civil War South.* Athens: University of Georgia Press, 2015.

Mitchell, Memory F. *Legal Aspects of Conscription and Exemption in North Carolina 1861–1865.* Chapel Hill: University of North Carolina Press, 1965.

Noe, Kenneth W. "'Alabama We Will Fight for Thee': The Initial Motivations of Later-enlisting Confederates," *Alabama Review* 62, no. 3 (July 2009): pp. 163–189.

_____. *Reluctant Rebels: The Confederates Who Joined the Army after 1861.* Chapel Hill: University of North Carolina Press, 2010.

Oates, John A. *The Story of Fayetteville.* Fayetteville, NC: Dowd Press, Third Edition, 1981.

Onion, Rebecca. "Dismantling the Myth of the 'Black Confederate,'" *Slate,* 30 August 2019. https://slate.com/human-interest/2019/08/black-confederate-myth-history-book.amp.

Raper, Horace W. "William W. Holden and the Peace Movement in North Carolina," *The North Carolina Historical Review* 31, no. 4 (1954): pp. 493–516. www.jstor.org/stable/23516160.

Reid, Richard. "A Test Case of the 'Crying Evil': Desertion Among North Carolina Troops During the Civil War," *The North Carolina Historical Review* 58, no. 3 (1981): pp. 234–62. www.jstor.org/stable/23534960.

Sears, Stephen W. *Chancellorsville.* New York: Houghton Mifflin, 1996.

_____. *Gettysburg.* New York: Houghton Mifflin, 2003.

Bibliography

_____. *Landscape Turned Red: The Battle of Antietam.* New York: Houghton Mifflin, 1983.

_____. *To the Gates of Richmond: The Peninsula Campaign.* New York: Ticknor & Fields, 1992.

Shaw, Cornelia Rebekah. *Davidson College.* New York: Fleming H. Revell Press, 1923.

Sheehan-Dean, Aaron. *Why Confederates Fought: Family & Nation in Civil War Virginia.* Chapel Hill: University of North Carolina Press, 2007.

Shepard, John, Jr. "Religion in the Army of Northern Virginia," *The North Carolina Historical Review* 25, no. 3 (1948): pp. 341–376.

Trotter, William R. *Ironclads and Columbiads: The Civil Wars in North Carolina, the Coast.* Winston-Salem, NC: John F. Blair, 1989.

_____. *Silk Flags and Cold Steel: The Civil War in North Carolina, the Piedmont.* Winston-Salem, NC: John F. Blair, 1988.

Van Zant, Jennifer. "Confederate Conscription and the North Carolina Supreme Court," *The North Carolina Historical Review* 72, no. 1 (1995): pp. 54–75. www.jstor.org/stable/23521870.

Venner, William Thomas. *The 30th North Carolina Infantry in the Civil War.* Jefferson, NC: McFarland, 2018.

Weitz, Mark A. "Drill, Training, and the Combat Performance of the Civil War Soldier: Dispelling the Myth of the Poor Soldier, Great Fighter," *The Journal of Military History* 62, no. 2 (April 1998): pp. 263–289.

Wellman, Manly Wade. *The County of Moore 1847–1947: A North Carolina Region's Second Hundred Years.* Southern Pines, NC: Moore County Historical Association, 1962.

"Western Railroad Company," *North Carolina Business History.* https://www.historync.org/railroad-WRR.htm.

Wheeler, Richard. *Sword Over Richmond: An Eyewitness History of McClellan's Peninsula Campaign.* New York: Harper, 1986.

Wingard, Timothy C. *The Mosquito: A Human History of Our Deadliest Predator.* New York: Dutton, 2019.

Woodward, Colin Edward. *Marching Masters: Slavery, Race, and the Confederate Army during the Civil War.* Charlottesville: University of Virginia Press, 2014.

Young, Alfred C., III. *Lee's Army During the Overland Campaign: A Numerical Study.* Baton Rouge: Louisiana State University Press, 2013.

Index

169

Index

furloughs 33, 34, 61, 110, 113, 114, 115, 116, 135, 155*n*21
furunulus 104

Gaines Mill, Battle of 62, 72, 88, 94, 95, 143*n*26, 152*n*6, 153*n*20
gangrene 96
Gaster, David 144*n*31
Gaster, Jacob 85
Gaster, Pvt. John C. 85
gastritis, acute 96
general debility 154*ch*9*n*4
geographical origins of recruits 53
George (enslaved man) 64
German measles 155*n*9
Gettysburg, Battle of 7, 32, 67, 68, 80, 136, 137, 144*n*31, 147*n*34, 150*n*36, 152*n*10, 156*n*40, 160*n*6
Gettysburg, Pennsylvania 65, 76
Gibraltar 54
Giuffre, Katherine 122
Glatthaar, Joseph T. 38, 40, 41, 43, 44, 46, 47, 48, 51
Goebel, Pvt. Charles 122
Goins, Pvt. Duncan 51, 66, 149*n*27
Goins, Pvt. Edward 51, 66, 149*n*28
Goins, William 51
gold mine miller 148*n*13
Goldsboro, North Carolina 9
gonorrhea 107, 154*ch*9*n*4
Goodin, Frances Brassfield 145*n*13
Goodin, Jesse B. 145*n*13, 160*n*6
Goodin, Pvt. John C. 31, 32, 107, 160*n*6
Goodin, Pvt. Joseph J. 31, 32, 125, 126, 128, 135, 160*n*6
Goodin, Pvt. Willis N. 31, 32, 117, 160*n*6
government clerks 35
Graham, Pvt. Jarratt 153*n*20
Graham, Pvt. Samuel 107, 155*n*28
Grant, Gen. U.S. 77, 128
Granville County, North Carolina 12, 61
Green, Capt. Joseph 19, 142*n*11
Green, Pvt. James L. 60, 125, 126
Griffin, Pvt. James 104, 155*n*24
Grissom, Capt. Eugene 32, 71, 141*n*13
Groves, Mary 23
Guilford County, North Carolina 127, 159*n*66
Gulf of Mexico 5

haematemesis 115
Hamilton's Crossing, Virginia 67, 75, 139*n*4

Harnett County, North Carolina 144*n*33
Harrell, Lt. George K. 124, 158*n*43
Harrington, Sgt. Abner Flynn 19, 20, 29, 31, 35, 37, 43, 64, 68, 75, 105, 118, 124, 126, 128, 143*n*15, 150*n*13
Harrington, Pvt. James Knox Polk 20, 31, 35, 64, 143*n*16
Harrington, James Stephens 35, 146*n*24
Harrington, John 33, 35, 64, 126
Harris, Hardy 18, 142*n*6
Harrisburg, Pennsylvania 152*n*9
Hatchels Mill, North Carolina 29
Hatteras Island, North Carolina 32
health of volunteers 94ff
heart disease 154*ch*9*n*4
heights of recruits 53
hemeralopia 102
hemorrhage of bowels 96
hemositis 115
Henry (an enslaved man) 63, 64; *see also* McLeod, Henry
hepatitis 114, 115; acute 114
hernias 96, 115, 154*ch*9*n*4
Hicks, Dick (free man of color) 66, 151*n*42
High Bridge, Virginia 144*n*31
Hill, Gen. A.P. 76
Hill, Gen. Daniel Harvey 7, 14, 15, 33, 67, 72, 134, 139*n*6, 147*n*1
Hilliard (an enslaved man) 66
Hinshaw, Pvt. Daniel 161*n*15
Holden, William W. 126
Holmes, Dr. Almond 124, 144*n*37
Holmes, Frances Sillers 144*n*37
Holmes, Capt. James C. 30, 33, 145*n*8
Holmes, Oliver Wendell 99
Hornaday, Pvt. Louis D. 102, 155*n*21
horse races 20
Hospital, Camp Winder Richmond, Virginia 85, 100
Hospital, Carver, Washington, D.C. 81
Hospital, Charlottesville, Virginia 61, 116
Hospital, Chimborazo Richmond, Virginia *see* Chimborazo Hospital
Hospital, Danville, Virginia 102
Hospital, Farmville, Virginia 102, 134
Hospital, General #9 Richmond, Virginia 149*n*26
Hospital, General #1, Richmond, Virginia 61
Hospital, General # 2, Richmond, Virginia 116
Hospital No. 5, Frederick, Maryland 81

172

173

Index

Index

Index